Praise for *STEAM Makers* by Jacie Maslyk

If your school is at the entry point of knowing that you need to begin providing opportunities for STEM education but are unsure of how to begin, *STEAM Makers: Fostering Creativity and Innovation in the Elementary Classroom* will quickly become your "go to" source. The author has done an amazing job of providing a mentor text that is written in a style that addresses the beginning questions of why to make time for this when faced with many demands for student improvement, as well as the realistic step-by-step guidance on how to implement.

In addition, if sharing with staff or colleagues, the writing style is one that the reader begins to feel that they are in the room talking with the author about STEAM, and because of this, it is hard to put down. While this is essential, the author also provides numerous resource options to continue to pick the text up as you undergo the implementation of STEAM in your school or classroom. This will not be a book that just sits on your shelf.

You will feel empowered and ready to provide these opportunities to your students after reading *STEAM Makers*.

—Jason Thompson
Assistant Principal
Jefferson Elementary, Schenectady, New York

STEAM Makers presents a crucial topic for educators who want to ensure that their students are prepared not to simply do well on tests but to be active participants in our rapidly changing economy. This book is a must-read for those who believe STEAM and making are important but may be overwhelmed by how to infuse this focus into their school culture. Upon completing this book, teachers will be prepared to open the minds of their students, increase critical thinking and motivation with even their most challenging students, and increase parent and community involvement in schools in a spectacular way.

—Nina Orellana
Title I/MTSS Coordinator
Palm Bay Academy Charter School, Palm Bay, Florida

STEAM Makers provides concrete evidence that the STEAM Maker movement will help our schools engage students in the lost art of learning through invention.

—Catherine Hernandez
Trashy Treasures Teacher
Detroit Public Schools, Detroit, Michigan

STEAM Makers connects the creativity of makers to the innovation of STEAM in the everyday classroom. This book is an excellent guide and resource for teachers and administrators to begin building making spaces in   ooms, school buildings, and school districts.

Tea

D1532597

STEAM Makers

To my Mom for inspiring me to write and
always telling me I could do anything I put my mind to.

STEAM Makers

Fostering Creativity and Innovation in the Elementary Classroom

Jacie Maslyk

A SAGE Publishing Company

FOR INFORMATION:

Corwin
A SAGE Company
2455 Teller Road
Thousand Oaks, California 91320
(800) 233-9936
www.corwin.com

SAGE Publications Ltd.
1 Oliver's Yard
55 City Road
London EC1Y 1SP
United Kingdom

SAGE Publications India Pvt. Ltd.
B 1/I 1 Mohan Cooperative Industrial Area
Mathura Road, New Delhi 110 044
India

SAGE Publications Asia-Pacific Pte. Ltd.
3 Church Street
#10-04 Samsung Hub
Singapore 049483

Senior Acquisitions Editor: Jessica Allan
Senior Associate Editor: Kimberly Greenberg
Editorial Assistant: Katie Crilley
Production Editor: Melanie Birdsall
Copy Editor: Karin Rathert
Typesetter: C&M Digitals (P) Ltd.
Proofreader: Annie Lubinsky
Indexer: Marilyn Augst
Cover Designer: Scott Van Atta
Marketing Manager: Margaret O'Connor

Photographs by Jacie Maslyk unless otherwise credited.

Printed in the United States of America

Library of Congress Cataloging-in-Publication Data

Names: Maslyk, Jacie.

Title: STEAM makers : fostering creativity and innovation in the elementary classroom / Jacie Maslyk.

Description: Thousand Oaks, California : Corwin/A SAGE Company, 2016. | Includes bibliographical references and index.

Identifiers: LCCN 2015039393 | ISBN 978-1-5063-1124-1 (pbk. : alk. paper)

Subjects: LCSH: Education, Elementary—Activity programs. | Creative activities and seat work. | Arts—Study and teaching (Elementary) | Science—Study and teaching (Elementary) | Interdisciplinary approach to education.

Classification: LCC LB1592 .M36 2016 | DDC 372.5/044—dc23 LC record available at http://lccn.loc.gov/2015039393

This book is printed on acid-free paper.

Certified Chain of Custody
Promoting Sustainable Forestry
www.sfiprogram.org
SFI-01268

SFI label applies to text stock

16 17 18 19 20 10 9 8 7 6 5 4 3 2 1

Contents

Preface

Depending on the decade in which you were born, you probably remember playing with Erector sets, Lincoln Logs, Legos, or K'NEX. You may have had a Lite Brite, Easy Bake Oven, or Shrinky Dinks. As a child, I remember building forts in my backyard, sewing blankets for my dolls, and growing vegetables in my grandfather's garden. "Kids have always made things—tree houses, skateboards, soapbox cars, doll houses, forts, and igloos" (Martinez & Stager, 2013, p. 29). This kind of learning is fun! These early childhood activities are a bridge connecting science, technology, engineering, art, and math.

John Dewey, philosopher and education reformer, advocated that students actively engage in authentic interdisciplinary projects connected to the real word. The implementation of STEAM and making embrace Dewey's thinking. Elementary schools across the country are exploring a variety of models as they infuse STEAM and making into their programs. This book will provide rich examples of the enthusiastic teaching and learning that is going on in innovative school districts. It is based on the idea that the Maker Movement combined with STEAM education empowers students and helps to build skills to create a more productive and sustainable global culture. *STEAM Makers* connect disciplines, bridging learning styles by naturally engaging young people as they apply learning in creative ways.

STEAM Making is gaining momentum across the country, but it is especially thriving in Pittsburgh, where there is a unique vibrancy. Pittsburgh is a place where formal and informal educators are working together to design unique learning pathways for children and young adults. Once a steel town known for blue-collar workers, Pittsburgh is still a city with a hard-working mentality. Now a cultural center embracing music and the arts, the city is home to theaters, museum, galleries, and makerspaces. Add the premier institutions of higher education and major corporations and Pittsburgh is poised to be a leading city of learning. Cathy Lewis Long, executive director and president of The Sprout Fund, says that Pittsburgh has a "secret sauce" (personal communication, March 2015) that makes the region a hot bed for innovation.

This year, the White House requested that Pittsburgh consider launching an "all hands on deck" (Kalil, 2015) effort to increase the number of the region's children with access to space, tools, mentors, and projects needed to design, create, and make. Since early in January 2015, city stakeholders, including civic leaders, foundations, educators, museum leaders, and researchers have been meeting to develop a learning ecosystem in an effort to motivate, inspire, and develop young people as they excel in STEAM through making.

Throughout my journey in writing this book, I had the opportunity to talk with educators at the leading edge of creativity and innovation. At networking events, school visits, and via Skype, I was able to learn about the tremendous efforts that schools are making toward the future. Each conversation led to more conversations at conferences, museums, libraries, and schools. Every chat with a maker, school principal, or superintendent led me to another organization or individual in the connected web of innovators. I learned so much from amazing educators working in K–8 classrooms and was completely inspired by the leadership from superintendents, assistant superintendents, directors of innovation, and principals who are supporting these practices in their schools. I was lifted up by the forward-thinking museum educators, foundation leaders, business owners, and those in higher education who are working to push this initiative to the forefront.

During my visit to the Grable Foundation, a major funder of innovative programs in Pittsburgh, executive director Gregg Behr succinctly summed up our common goal: "We need to think differently about educating young people. We need to light them up on a learning pathway." STEAM Making is a way to show young people the possible learning pathway, while also allowing them to create their own.

Schools haven't really changed much over the last 100 years. Students have progressed through each grade traversing through a fairly traditional curriculum, taking the required assessments. If we are now looking to "light up" our students on a pathway to the future, perhaps we need to consider some new routes. Gregg Behr suggested "a concierge in their life to direct them on whatever their pathway is." Perhaps you are the concierge to a young maker or a group of students. Consider the ways that you might support them on their STEAM Making journey.

Acknowledgments

This book would not exist without the amazing people at Crafton Elementary School. The teachers, staff, parents, and community have been a tremendous support as we have worked together to light up a pathway toward creativity and innovation for our students.

Thank you to everyone in the Remake Learning Network—the epitome of what it means to be collaborative. I am grateful to all of the educators, formal and informal, who gave their time and ideas to this work.

A special thanks to my family and friends for their ongoing encouragement. To my beautiful boys, Caden and Tanner, thank you for being patient while I wrote this book. Most of all I want to thank my husband and teammate Christian, for always supporting me and my commitment to education.

PUBLISHER'S ACKNOWLEDGMENTS

Corwin gratefully acknowledges the contributions of the following reviewers:

Dr. Patricia Allanson
Instructor
Deltona Middle School
Deltona, FL

Regina Brinker
Science Teacher
Granada High School
Livermore, CA

Randy Cook
Teacher
Tri County High School
Howard City, MI

Hope Edlin
Teacher
Bethel Elementary School
Simpsonville, SC

Mandy Frantti
Teacher
Munising High School
Munising, MI

Catherine Hernandez
Trashy Treasures Teacher
Detroit Public Schools
Detroit, MI

About the Author

Studio Ten

Jacie Maslyk, EdD, has served in public education over the past nineteen years. During that time, she has served in many roles. As a classroom teacher and reading specialist, she worked in both inner city and suburban school districts. She served as an elementary school principal and director of elementary education for the last ten years, with extensive experience in curriculum, assessment, and instruction. A successful school leader, she was recognized as a National Distinguished Principal finalist in Pennsylvania in 2013 and 2014. Recently, Dr. Maslyk has been named the assistant superintendent of the Hopewell Area School District.

The author served as an editorial advisor for the National Association of Elementary School Principals (NAESP) *Principal Magazine*, contributing to several articles. In addition, she has published a number of articles on Response to Intervention and Instruction, school leadership, the Common Core, STEAM education, and the Maker Movement. In 2015, she was awarded the Frank S. Manchester Award for Excellence in Journalism from the Pennsylvania Association of Elementary and Secondary School Principals (PAESSP). She has made dozens of presentations at the local, state, and national level at various conferences and workshops. She presented on STEAM at the annual conference for the National Board for Professional Teaching Standards.

The author is also involved in a variety of STEAM and making initiatives in the field of education. She served on the advisory board for the Mobile MAKESHOP® at the Pittsburgh Children's Museum and led one of the first elementary schools serving as a mobile maker site. She is also on the Spark Advisory Committee for the Sprout Fund, a national organization that supports innovative ideas and provides funds for catalyzing change in the areas of creativity, innovation, and cultivating connected communities.

Introduction

There is a current disconnect in our educational system. Eric Sheninger speaks about it in his recent book, *Digital Leadership* (2014). He calls for a transformation that will turn schools into vibrant places for learning that unleash student creativity and open new pathways to innovation. One pathway is the integration of relevant, engaging learning for students in science, technology, engineering, and math (STEM).

Educators are under pressure to increase the amount of integrated STEM content taught to students (National Research Council, 2011), but few teachers have had significant opportunities to learn and develop the skills necessary to provide this instruction. During the next decade, U.S. demand for scientists and engineers is expected to increase at four times the rate for all other occupations!

In order to equip future leaders with the necessary skills to power innovation and economic growth, students must be more than proficient readers and writers, they must be literate in science, technology, engineering, art, and math. Schools, libraries, community groups, and institutions of higher education are beginning to observe this trend and infuse new opportunities into their programming.

These types of programs have increased student skills in the 4C's: creativity, collaboration, communication, and critical thinking. Often called 21st Century Skills, these are future-facing dispositions that young people need to possess. (Since we are fifteen-plus years into this century, we should probably call these skills something else.)

Subjects in school cannot be addressed in isolation. The integration of concepts is an important prerequisite for students going to college and entering careers. Innovation is not exclusive to scientists, programmers, and engineers; it requires input from artists, designers, and creative problem solvers as well. Tapping into innovation and creativity, STEM has shifted to STEAM, adding the *A* for the arts.

Elementary students are naturally curious and often willing to engage in new ideas. Implementing STEAM and making at this level is a natural fit for students at this age. These types of learning experiences can be powerful learning opportunities for children. STEAM and making are on a rising trajectory.

Some schools have redesigned spaces within their buildings; others revamped their curriculum to include programming, robotics, and digital media. Young learners need to engage in authentic tasks: brainstorming, setting goals, gathering materials, sketching, questioning, constructing, and fixing things, which can happen in and out of schools.

STEAM-Makers

To read a QR code, you must have a smartphone or tablet with a camera. We recommend that you download a QR code reader app that is made specifically for your phone or tablet brand.

It is my hope that this book will provide a background in what I call STEAM Making, while providing guidance to make these instructional shifts. To help readers find inspiration in the schools and organizations that are already engaging in this exciting work, links and resource lists have been interspersed throughout the book. In addition, a website has been set up at **www.STEAM-Makers.com** as well as a Pinterest account at **https://www.pinterest.com/jaciemaslyk/steam-makers**, where you can access additional resources.

Pinterest

Chapter 1 will provide a brief history of STEM and its transformation into STEAM. The Maker Movement will be discussed as well as the mindset needed to engage in this type of work. The connection between the two forms the integrated model of learning called STEAM Making.

The reality of the Common Core and the Next Generation Science Standards will also be aligned to the STEAM Makers model.

In Chapter 2, the changes in STEAM Making are reviewed, including the impact at the district, school, and classroom level. We will look at schools that have embraced changes in culture, curriculum, and physical space. Innovative schools and organizations will be highlighted.

Chapter 3 hits on the important theme of failure. Developing the Habits of Mind and the Engineering Habits of Mind establish the characteristics needed in learners. Assessment is discussed in this chapter, with an emphasis on badging. STEAM Making is an all-inclusive practice that can positively impact all types of learners. Examples will be shared regarding students with learning disabilities, speech and language impairments, and those with autism. Stories about several student STEAM Makers are shared within this chapter, as well.

Creating connections between STEAM and making is explored in Chapter 4. This chapter will highlight the journey of one elementary school as it transformed its programming and developed a dedicated makerspace for K–6 students. Student stories and teacher challenges will be shared throughout the chapter. Numerous resources developed by the school are also included.

In Chapter 5, the concept of building will be explored. Schools and districts are building physical learning spaces. They are building new programs and curriculum to meet the needs of their students. District leaders are building a culture for the STEAM Maker movement, a culture that promotes growth and design thinking. We will share stories from amazing schools like The Ellis School, Elizabeth Forward School District, Kiski Intermediate School, and the South Fayette School District.

The importance of creating a STEAM Maker network is shared in Chapter 6. The work of Pittsburgh's Remake Learning is highlighted along with the learning ecosystem that is being nurtured within this region. Stories from innovative organizations within the Remake Learning network are provided to show the possibilities of learning partners. The Millvale Community Library, Assemble, and the Allegheny Intermediate Unit will be highlighted. Expanding the network to higher education, new ideas will be shared from the Center for Arts and Education at West Liberty University and Robert Morris University.

Chapter 7 will provide some tools to help anyone start their STEAM Making journey. We will discuss planning for student engagement and the importance of connecting to local experts. In-text tools will help readers to focus on an action plan, including getting resources and pursuing grants funds to support STEAM Making.

NOTE FROM THE PUBLISHER

The author has provided video and web content throughout the book that is available to you through QR codes. To read a QR code, you must have a smartphone or tablet with a camera. We recommend that you download a QR code reader app that is made specifically for your phone or tablet brand.

CHAPTER 1

Learn

Anyone who stops learning is old, whether at twenty or eighty. Anyone who keeps learning stays young.

—Henry Ford

Imagine a school where students build the classroom furniture, design outdoor landscapes, launch rockets, and create inventions to improve everyday life. What if school learning spaces were designed with comfortable corners for collaboration and areas to foster informal learning? What if students were given the opportunity to learn what they wanted to, pursuing their own interests within the school day? This is happening in elementary classrooms across the country! There is a shift occurring in education that has the potential to transform teaching and learning. With roots that date back to Dewey, Montessori, and Piaget, there is a movement for schools to return creativity and hands-on learning to the classroom, a belief that learning should be active and with students constructing their own knowledge.

While the accountability pressures on schools don't seem to be going away anytime soon, educators are embracing the idea of a school culture that emphasizes learning by doing. From the early 1900s through present day, student-centered learning has been a part of educational practice. President Barack Obama has taken notice of this renewed concept, stating, "I want us all to think about new and creative ways to engage young people in science and engineering, whether it's science festivals, robotics competitions, fairs that encourage young people to create and build and invent—to be makers of things, not just consumers of things" (Schulman, 2013). The events the President is suggesting are the types of opportunities that are beginning to occur in innovative schools across the country. The notion of citizens as makers, not consumers, connects to the mindset that is growing the Maker Movement and STEAM education.

There may be some resistance to this approach, especially with ongoing accountability pressures facing schools. With any change in practice comes excitement paired with anxiety and challenge mixed with uncertainty. Despite the push for rigorous content and standardized assessments, many schools are forging ahead with efforts to include STEAM and *making* into their practices. STEAM Making is experimental and playful at times, but it connects critical academic content as well. As an instructional practice, STEAM Making represents the belief of new possibilities. These possibilities, presented to children, allow them to engage in the process of creating, designing, and pursuing learning that is interesting to them and has value outside of the school walls.

STEAM Making provides the opportunity for kids to get creative, collaborate, and engage in learning that is both challenging and fun. People outside of education are talking about these new ideas and the ways that they can infuse new life into schools and communities. The mayor of Pittsburgh recently opened his Maker Movement Roundtable by saying, "We are at the forefront of something pretty large, not only in this country but around the world." *U.S. News & World Report* summed it up best by saying, this initiative is "just getting started"! (**http://www.usnews.com/ news/stem-solutions/articles/2014/02/13/gaining-steam-teaching -science-though-art**).

U.S. News & World Report

A 2008 study titled "Ready to Innovate" revealed that more and more companies are looking for skills in their new employees that involve creativity rather than achievement in core subjects alone. The study reported that companies want workers who can brainstorm, problem solve, collaborate creatively, and communicate new ideas. These aren't the skills of the 21st century. They are the skills of right now! Similarly, a collaboration of The Conference Board, Corporate Voices for Working Families, the Partnership for 21st Century Skills, and the Society for Human Resource Management (2006) compiled a report titled *Are They Really Ready to Work?* and stated, "Among the most important applied skills cited by employers are professionalism and work ethic, oral and written communications, teamwork and collaboration, and critical thinking and problem solving." We must ask ourselves if our current educational practices are preparing our graduates for this future.

HISTORY OF STEM

Many point to the Sputnik and the Space Race as the turning point for science education in the United States. Others connect the turning point to poor science and math scores by U.S. students, as highlighted by *A Nation at Risk* (U.S. National Commission on Excellence in Education, 1983). Now driven by business demands and the economy, STEM learning has been a prominent buzzword in education.

In the early 2000s, The National Science Foundation (NSF) coined the term STEM: learning based on the idea that science, technology, engineering, and math are interrelated and should be taught in an integrated way. Traditional teaching in these subjects is often presented as a silo model, with each being taught in isolation, which prevents students from seeing the connections between the content learned in these areas.

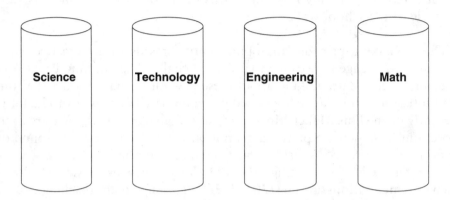

Throughout middle and high school, I struggled with math. It didn't matter which course, every single one was a challenge for me. I hated Algebra II. I barely passed geometry, and forget trigonometry. I remember staring blankly at equations and formulas and wondering to myself, "When am I ever going to use this again?" Since my math courses were entirely textbook driven, I never really saw math's connection to anything else. My teachers never gave any real-world examples. "Tonight, everyone will do the odd numbered problems" was a standard assignment.

Science was another story. While I wasn't convinced that dissecting sheep hearts was entirely my thing, I loved chemistry, astronomy, and earth science. These subjects led me to question things, experiment, wonder about possibilities, and think like a scientist. I had teachers who presented science as connected content, making meaningful connections to real life. These classes were tough, but the nature of discovery learning kept my attention.

I wonder what would have happened if my teachers had connected their subject matter together. Would I (and other students) have been more successful in math? Would an integrated approach have made more sense? Would the connections between math and science have led us to see the connections in other areas and to the world? While we can't live in a world of what-ifs, I believe that my high school grade point average would have inched a little higher had a STEM approach been implemented back in the '80s and '90s.

WHO NEEDS A JOB?

Integrated STEM learning is becoming a requirement to create the kind of workforce needed in the United States and across the globe. Schools are responding by creating STEM courses, after-school clubs, and summer camps. Others are revamping departments and restructuring curriculum to meet these demands. Some schools are even reinventing themselves as STEM-focused schools and academies.

On the main page of STEM Education News (**http://www.stemeducation news.com**) this statistic jumps out: "By 2018 there will be 1.2 million job openings in science, technology, engineering, and math (STEM) fields. Due to a significant projected shortage of qualified applicants, many of these will go unfilled. The job market is demanding students increase their knowledge in STEM fields. In order to prepare students for this future, STEM education is building rapidly and transforming as it progresses."

STEM Education News

While some critics see STEM as a fad that will soon fade away, others believe this is a powerful vehicle to prepare our students for the global challenges in their future. As we know in education, though, things don't remain the same for very long. Once the importance for STEM was established, the idea began to transform.

ADDING THE *A*

Not long after STEM took hold, educators began altering the original concept. Obsessed with acronyms in education, STEM has morphed into STEM-X, TEAMS, STEAM, STEAMIE, and STREAM. At a recent conference, a colleague mentioned that one school was now using the term HAMSTER: Humanities, Art, Math, Science, Technology, Engineering, and Reading. Jesse Schell, CEO of video game design company Schell Games, warns educators of this very thing. "If you just start adding everything in there, then you are left with nothing. Nothing important" (personal communication, January 27, 2015). So, we need to ensure that we are making meaningful connections between subject areas in a way that prepares students for the real-world experiences that they will face once they leave the school setting.

In *The STEAM Journal*, Henriksen writes, "STEAM must become an essential paradigm for creative and artistically infused teaching and learning in the sciences" (2014, p. 1). I would argue that STEAM is a meaningful spin-off, especially in the elementary grades. The integration of arts into the STEM fields takes learning to a whole new level. The arts help to develop creativity, imagination, and collaboration (Sousa & Pilecki, 2013). Adding these components to STEM learning enhances the existing opportunities for critical thinking, problem solving, and communication. By allowing for creativity and critical thinking, teaching and learning move away from convergent thinking to divergent thinking. But beware—this is hard for teachers! Fostering divergent thinking means that there is no longer one correct answer to every problem. It means that we need to look beyond the manual and the answer key and encourage kids to come up with their own questions and answers.

Henrisken (2014) also suggests that arts-based teaching leads to more motivated, engaged, and effective learning in STEM subjects. Adding the *A* to STEM doesn't mean just art. It is not an add-on that is merely decorative (Beckman, 2010). The arts should be an essential part of the process and could encompass drawing, painting, sculpting, music, movement, and video, just to name a few. In their book, *Invent to Learn* (2013), Sylvia Libow Martinez and Gary Stager state, "Combining the arts with STEAM means that children can express themselves in even more variations" (p. 55). The arts provide numerous creative pathways to learning. In their book *From STEM to STEAM*, Sousa & Pilecki (2013) share research-based reasons to integrate the arts:

- Engage the brain and develop cognitive growth

- Improve long-term memory

- Promote creativity

- Reduce stress

One of our goals should be to break down the barriers between creative subjects like art and music and more traditional subjects like science and math. This infusion of subjects will support learning for those that are creative AND logical-mathematical, unlike the silo model that isolates these topics. Developing creativity by integrating the arts makes a huge impact on student learning. The multisensory, hands-on nature that the arts can bring to STEM lessons helps students to connect to the content. Learning becomes more personal when students include an artistic component. An artistic representation of ideas and solutions is a valuable way to make learning personal. Infusing the arts may allow students to envision things in a different way.

LEFT BRAIN VERSUS RIGHT BRAIN

Are you left-brain or right-brain oriented? How about your students? Left brainers possess strengths in sequential thinking and critical details. These learners are logical, analytical, and driven by facts. For them, traditional teaching in science, technology, engineering, and math make sense. Those with inclinations toward the right brain are more creative in nature. They don't think in a linear fashion. Some may be daydreamers, letting their imaginations run wild. This group is visual and artistic. STEM learning works just fine for left-brain learners, but often excludes those that are creative and artistic. STEAM embraces the arts and provides opportunities for both sides of the brain to engage. After all, shouldn't a well-rounded student develop both sides of the brain? Students can develop strategies and define patterns (left brain), and represent ideas spatially through color and design (right brain) all within a STEAM Making lesson.

WHAT EDUCATORS ARE SAYING

In a recent Google Hangout, participants pondered the shift from STEM to STEAM (**https://www.youtube.com/watch?v=GpaolpSxBZE &feature=youtu.be**).

Google Hangout

Educators from across the eastern United States talked about what makes STEAM different. These thought leaders from public and independent schools started by explaining the need for the *A*. They talked about the inclusion of the arts as a key element for bridging the learning that happens in traditional STEM courses and making it accessible to all learners. They stressed the importance of design thinking in K–12 education, urging others to talk with their students about problems and solutions and their ability to help someone or something by designing an innovative solution.

During the hangout three major themes emerged:

- The opportunity for creativity and originality

- The importance of perseverance through iterations

- The need to give and receive feedback in the process

While the focus of the discussion was STEAM education, these educators continued to stray away from using specific terms like STEM and STEAM to talk more about making in general. There is real overlap between the two. They described the work (no matter what name we give it: STEAM, making, hands-on learning, PBL [project-based learning]) as difficult. A STEAM teacher from a northeastern independent school explained that it takes patience and resilience. She shared what the students were making in her math class. In a spin-off of a traditional lesson on tessellations, her fifth- and sixth-grade students are now using laser cutters to create their own tessellations. The students are then using those manipulatives to teach their younger peers in kindergarten and first grade.

Schools are embracing the idea of STEAM education, with an emphasis on the *A*. This approach to instruction provides all types of learners with an entry point into challenging content that connects with life beyond the school walls. The *A* is where STEAM and making intersect. It is at this crossroads where student engagement soars. It is the place where teachers and students have that "aha" moment; the aha that they are learning, when they think that all they are doing is "playing." While some makers may disagree and some scientists may balk at the idea of adding the artistic component to their left-brain thinking, these two practices connect in a number of ways, creating a promising alignment between STEAM and the Maker Movement.

On her blog User Generated Education (**https://usergeneratededucation .wordpress.com/2013/07/23/steam-and-maker-education-inclusive-engaging-self-differentiating**), Jackie Gerstein stated, "Maker education activities make for a beautiful integration of STEAM." In their classrooms, libraries, studios, and makerspaces, it is this "beautiful integration" that schools are discovering. STEAM supports right-brain thinking that includes imagining and risk taking, which are both critical tenets behind the Maker Movement.

User Generated Education

THE MAKER MOVEMENT

Whether it's remodeling and flipping houses, selling homemade goods on Etsy, or crafting items that were inspired by pins on Pinterest, people *are* making. Society is in a do-it-yourself era, which is only being fast-tracked through the use of technology. The Maker Movement has been sweeping across the nation in big cities, small communities, school systems, and online. This return to DIY (do-it-yourself), hands-on creating has spurred its own magazine, initiated makerspaces in libraries and community centers, and altered the way schools are looking at learning.

Make Magazine

In 2005, the Maker Movement gained momentum when Dale Daugherty launched *Make* magazine (**http://makezine.com**). The magazine has connected people from a variety of disciplines and developed a common ground for making. The following year, the first Maker Faire© was held in San Francisco. A venue for crafters, tinkerers, and programmers, this event has continued each year, expanding to more and more cities. In the January 2014 edition of *The New Yorker*, Evgeny Morozov called Maker Faire© a "celebration of the DIY mind-set."

Maker Education Initiative

The celebration of making is spreading as organizations, foundations, and grassroots groups are popping up across the globe. The Maker Education Initiative (MEI) (**http://makered .org**) is one that works to build confidence, foster creativity, and spark interest in science, technology, engineering, math, and the arts, while creating opportunities in making. Their mission is to provide resources to educators so that they are able to facilitate meaningful making experiences. MEI builds capacity within organizations so that young people can engage in making in both formal and informal environments. MEI seeks to equip communities so that kids and young adults from any background have access to making opportunities. The Maker Movement aligns with the need to increase STEAM education, as making embraces a similar philosophy of generating new ideas, engaging in hands-on/minds-on work, collaborating, and the integration of different fields.

Conversations are happening across the country to find meaningful ways to integrate STEAM and making into the daily work of educators and those who work with children and young adults. Formal conversations in offices and schools and informal conversations on Twitter and other social media are pushing this idea forward as well. (Check out #makered, #makerspaces, #makermovment, #STEAM, or #edtech on Twitter.) Elementary, middle, and high schools are creating unique spaces within their schools to develop STEAM learning and opportunities for students to engage in making. Libraries and community centers are welcoming artists, designers, and programmers into their buildings to provide hands-on activities not usually experienced in these spaces. Schools of higher education are paying attention too and are beginning to include STEM courses their teacher education programs. Some are embracing the concept even further, opening "makerspaces" on their campuses.

WHAT DOES MAKING LOOK LIKE IN SCHOOLS?

Find It! (Space)

Making can happen just about anywhere, but lots of schools are creating makerspaces or mobile making carts to facilitate these practices. Wherever the space—a room, the hallway, or outside—it needs to be accessible to everyone. Large or small, simple or complex, many schools are finding the library to be a good fit. Laura Fleming's book *Worlds of Making: Best Practices for Establishing a Makerspace for Your School* is part of the Corwin Connected Educators Series and is a great resource for those interested in starting a makerspace. As a library media specialist, she transformed the library at New Milford High School in New Jersey into an engaging space for her students.

STEAM Maker Storage

More STEAM Maker Storage

Learning Space

Learning Space

Fill It! (Materials)

With a large budget, you can buy all the latest machines and gadgets, but you can start making with little or no budget at all. Most schools already have the basics to start making: a couple of computers, tables and chairs, empty boxes, paper, scissors, glue. With parent and community donations, smaller items can be easily added, such as fabric scraps, buttons, needles, thread, old magazines, cardboard, plastic containers, and simple hand tools (hammer, screwdriver, etc.). With some funding, add sewing machines, hot glue guns, soldering irons, batteries, and motors.

A supply list to get you started is in Appendix E. (Also, read how Avonworth Elementary engaged parents and community members and stocked their makerspace in Chapter 2.)

Staff It! (People)

Providing access to making is important, but who is going to do all that work? Some schools have the ability to assign a full-time staff member to the makerspace or learning studio. Most schools will not be that fortunate. Building expertise among teachers is key, but this takes time. Providing professional development is one way to start. (Appendix B shows a sample professional development schedule that one school used to support teacher learning over the course of a year.)

Another way to build knowledge is through parents and community members. Can a parent who has a background in carpentry talk with students about safety in woodworking? Maybe a local architect could come in to provide a "lunch and learn" session with students to talk about their career? Could a group of moms who know how to knit or sew start a club for interested students? Tapping into parents as a resource is not only a free way to build expertise but also a way to build positive momentum for your program. If parents value this type of learning, they will help to promote the work that is happening at your school.

1. Everyone can be good at something.
2. They promote high levels of student engagement.
3. Learning opportunities are concrete, hands-on, and multisensory, meeting the needs of *all* learners.
4. Processes focus on the learning by doing, not merely the end product.
5. Open-ended tasks lead to higher-level questions.
6. Students (and teachers) learn that failure can be OK.

THE MINDSET

Embracing STEAM Making does require a certain mindset. There is a lot of discussion in education right now about the growth mindset. Carol Dweck (2006) defines the growth mindset as the power of believing you can improve. Some students (and teachers) have a fixed mindset, one that prevents them from growing and learning in the face of challenges. The belief that abilities can be nurtured and developed is clear inside classrooms and schools that embrace STEAM and making. In Dweck's 2014 TED Talk she emphasizes the importance of teaching our students that they *can* get smarter. It is that can-do attitude that needs to be present as we adjust our practices and integrate creativity into our classrooms.

A mindset to support STEAM Making can be defined within the four Ps:

- People
- Personalization
- Persistence
- Play

In schools where STEAM and making are growing, it is due to the **people:** teachers, principals, superintendents, and other school leaders who are fostering this mindset. STEAM and making thrive, not just because of the people leading it but because of the sharing and collaboration that happen among makers. When young people and adults are engaged in making, they share expertise and connect with others. This connection happens face to face in makerspaces but also online through a growing community of bloggers, "pinners," and "Twitterers."

STEAM and making are strategies that make sense for different types of learners. **Personalization** makes that possible. The hands-on nature of this work lends itself to true student-centered learning. When students have a choice in what they are working on, engagement is high and students are focused. Enter a makerspace and watch students as they select materials or work on projects. Their personal interests drive their decision making. (You'll hear from students in Chapter 4 as they describe why personalization transformed their interest in school.) Traditional teaching and learning place teachers at the front of the room delivering content to students. When learning is made personal, the teacher can facilitate individual interests and foster the work initiated by children.

How often do you set your students up to fail? Probably not a question you've been asked before! Failure will be discussed more in Chapter 3, but it is an important component of **persistence**. Acquiring knowledge in STEAM Making comes through inquiry and exploration, as opposed to direct instruction or mastery learning. This takes time and effort.

Take a design challenge, for example. Students are given some materials, criteria for building, and time to work. The design process requires them to devise a plan—a plan that may or may not work. The plan may be revised or completely thrown out the window. The students might try several iterations of a model to meet the design criteria. This work can be frustrating for kids, especially for those who need instant gratification and validation. (Does this cover many of the kids that you know?) Developing a maker mindset means that teachers and students build qualities of perseverance and persistence in the face of challenges.

The last P is for **play**. STEAM learning and making are fun approaches to classroom instruction. Tasks tap into student curiosity and allow creativity to shine. Student makers tinker and explore with a variety of materials in a variety of spaces. STEAMers build and design in ways that challenge the mind and brighten the spirit. STEAM Makers combine to form a model of learning that is truly student centered and fun.

Things You Will Never Hear Coming From a Classroom That Embraces STEAM Making

Students

- "Why do I have to learn this?"
- "Am I ever going to use this again?"
- "Do I have to do this for homework?"
- "This is boring!"

Educators

- "My students aren't engaged."
- "He just won't pay attention."
- "Those students keep misbehaving."
- "This class isn't motivated to do anything!"

I'm not trying to say that *every* problem disappears when you engage students in STEAM Making, but many traditional problems do fade away. Keep in mind, they are replaced with new problems:

Students

- "Can't we do this project all day long?"
- "I need more materials to build my rocket."
- "Johnny won't let me use the soldering iron!"
- "I can't figure out how to add sounds to my animation."

Educators

- "My students want to learn how to _____ and I need some training."
- "I need a venue for my students to present their projects to the community."
- "We are inundated with recyclable materials and need more storage solutions."

IS IT PROJECT-BASED LEARNING?

Andrew Miller's 2014 post on Edutopia calls STEAM and making "a natural fit with project-based learning" (**http://www.edutopia .org/blog/pbl-and-steam-natural-fit-andrew-miller**).

Edutopia

All of these types of learning emphasize the process over the product. It is the actual learning that is important! When combining these ideas together the importance of integrated learning, real-world connections, and authentic work shine through.

If project-based learning is a collaborative and student-centered approach to learning, then it is a great fit with STEAM Making. It offers students the opportunity to engage in complex problem-solving tasks that often build on prior knowledge. These tasks require critical thinking and other skills needed for students to be successful in college, careers, and beyond.

Through PBL, students build competencies valuable for today's world. PBL allows students to engage in in-depth inquiry, asking questions, using resources, and developing answers. Projects are often focused on a driving question. Students can generate one that captures their interest and prompts exploration.

With students driving this learning, curiosity is nurtured and the voice of the student is honored. Led by student choice, PBL includes students in the assessment process as well. Learning to give and receive feedback on the quality of their work and making revisions are a critical part of PBL. Communicating about their learning beyond the teacher is encouraged in PBL. Sharing with the community or globally through technology can be incorporated in project-based learning.

Buck Institute for Education

The Buck Institute for Education (BIE) is a resource that provides teaching tools, curriculum materials, professional development courses, relevant research, and numerous student handouts to guide PBL in the classroom. Check out its website (**http://bie.org/about**).

Will Richardson

At a recent Research Institute Summit, Will Richardson, author, speaker, and well-respected educational blogger, addressed the group about learning (**http://willrichardson.com**). He questioned all of the descriptors that often accompany the word learning: problem-based learning, inquiry-based learning, 21st century learning. Each has had their place in the cycle (and recycle) of educational practices. Richardson argues that it should boil down to simply—*learning*.

WHY IS THIS IMPORTANT?

Twenty-first century students want active, relevant learning. They want to be connected to their peers, those in and out of school. They want to pursue their interests and have a choice in their learning. While this may be out of the comfort zone for some educators, there are many potential benefits to implementing this in the classroom. As we know, success beyond school requires more than basic knowledge and skills. Want students to understand content more deeply? Want them to retain what they've learned? Interested in seeing them build their confidence and solve complex problems? If we want to truly reach our students and help them to become thinkers, questioners, and innovators, then this is worth a shot.

BUT WHAT ABOUT STATE TESTING AND THE COMMON CORE?

Let's face it, if it's not PARCC (Partnership for Assessment of Readiness for College and Careers), Smarter Balanced or some assessment developed by our state department, it will be something else. While it is tempting to let these distractions lead us to teach to the test and overwhelm our students with test prep workbooks, worksheets, and practice tests before the actual test, at some point we need to ask ourselves, What is really best for kids? Do we want to create a generation of good test takers? Do we want students who can click on a circle with proficiency? Or do we want students who can think for themselves, communicate with others, and successfully work with a team?

The Common Core State Standards' (CCSS) emphasis on real-world application of knowledge and skills, push for competencies in critical thinking, use of relevant technology and media, and focus on student collaboration fit well within the framework for STEAM education and the Maker Movement (see Table 1.1). The rigor and relevance that these newly adopted standards require can be addressed through hands-on/ minds-on learning that happens in schools embracing STEAM Making. Students develop an in-depth content knowledge of the material they are learning about. They focus on the process of completing a task, not just the product. Engaging in problem-solving tasks, students learn how to reason and persevere when the answers are not right there in front of them. These experiences offer students the opportunity to build independence but also work collaboratively with others. The CCSS require students to investigate topics, analyze data, cite evidence, and present information. Isn't this what we want our graduates to do?

Since STEAM and making take an integrated approach to learning, students gain a more comprehensive understanding of topics and how the topics relate to the real world. The CCSS aren't the only standards that need to be considered, though. The Next Generation Science Standards released in 2013 also align with STEAM and making.

NEXT GENERATION SCIENCE STANDARDS

With the release of the Next Generation Science Standards (NGSS), this is a critical time to engage students in STEAM fields. "Science, engineering, and technology permeate nearly every facet of modern life, and they also hold the key to meeting many of humanity's most pressing current and future challenges" (National Research Council, 2013).

The NGSS include a framework for science learning that includes components of STEAM and making and was developed through a partnership between the National Research Council (NRC), National Science Teachers Association (NSTA), American Association for the Advancement of Science (AAAS), and Achieve (an educational, nonprofit reform organization). Twenty-six states collaborated with these partners to create them. These standards recommend that science be built around the following three major dimensions: (1) scientific and engineering practices, (2) crosscutting concepts, and (3) core areas.

Scientific and Engineering Practices

Scientists engage in certain practices as they investigate the world around them. Engineers also employ these practices as they design and build models. A strong foundation of both skills and knowledge are needed to develop these practices. With an emphasis on engineering, the NGSS stress the formulation of problems that can be solved through design. It is this type of learning that will clarify for students the relevance of science, technology, engineering and mathematics beyond school.

What does this look like in the classroom?

- Students asking questions as they plan and carrying out investigations

- Learners developing and using models to solve real problems

- Classrooms engaged in gathering, analyzing, and interpreting data as they construct explanations and design solutions

- Groups of students engaging in computational thinking and using evidence to build and defend an argument

Crosscutting Concepts

The NGSS define the crosscutting concepts as those that have application across all domains of science. These include patterns; cause and effect; scale, proportion, and quantity; systems; energy and matter; structure and function; and stability and change. Not only do some of these concepts have application in science and engineering, but they also have application in math, technology, and the arts.

Core Areas

The core areas, as defined by NGSS, are made up of physical science; life science; earth and space science; and engineering, technology, and application. These areas were selected because they are important across multiple disciplines. Within the general curriculum, these domains are taught over multiple grade levels at increasing levels of depth.

The three dimensions of the NGSS provide a framework for the K–12 standards in science and engineering, but combined with the CCSS, these also align with the four components of STEAM and the mindset for makers. The connection to the CCSS includes not only the Standards for Mathematical Practice but also the individual standards from within the English Language Arts Standards (reading, writing, speaking, and listening).

This is by no means a comprehensive analysis and alignment of the standards but rather intends to show the multiple connections between the two sets of standards and their alignment with the principles of STEAM and maker

TABLE 1.1 Correlations of Standards

NEXT GENERATION SCIENCE STANDARDS: SCIENTIFIC AND ENGINEERING PRACTICES	COMMON CORE STATE STANDARDS	ALIGNMENT WITH STEAM AND MAKER MINDSET
1. Asking questions (for science) and defining problems (for engineering)	**Speaking and Listening:** Prepare for and participate effectively in a range of conversations and collaborations with diverse partners, building on others' ideas and expressing their own clearly and persuasively.	Personalization
2. Developing and using models	**Standards for Mathematical Practice:** Model with mathematics.	Persistence
3. Planning and carrying out investigations	**Standards for Mathematical Practice:** Look for and express regularity in repeated reasoning.	Playful
4. Analyzing and interpreting data	**Standards for Mathematical Practice:** Look for and make use of structure. **Standards for Mathematical Practice:** Reason abstractly and quantitatively.	Persistence
5. Using mathematics and computational thinking	**Standards for Mathematical Practice:** Make sense of problems and persevere in solving them. **Standards for Mathematical Practice:** Attend to precision.	Persistence
6. Constructing explanations (for science) and designing solutions (for engineering)	**Speaking and Listening:** Present information, findings, and supporting evidence such that listeners can follow the line of reasoning and the organization, development, and style are appropriate to task, purpose, and audience. **Standards for Mathematical Practice:** Construct viable arguments and critique the reasoning of others.	Playful
7. Engaging in argument from evidence	**Writing:** Write arguments to support claims in an analysis of substantive topics or texts, using valid reasoning and relevant and sufficient evidence. **Reading:** Delineate and evaluate the argument and specific claims in a text, including the validity of the reasoning as well as the relevance and sufficiency of the evidence.	People
8. Obtaining, evaluating, and communicating information	**Writing:** Gather relevant information from multiple print and digital sources, assess the credibility and accuracy of each source, and integrate the information while avoiding plagiarism.	People

education. As you develop learning opportunities in STEAM and making in your school, you will certainly find additional connections to relevant standards.

WHAT DOES IT MEAN TO BE CREATIVE IN A STANDARDS-BASED SYSTEM?

Young children are instinctively creative: building with blocks, finger painting, using their imaginations, and exploring the world around them. STEAM education and the practice of making embraces this idea and enhances creativity beyond the general curriculum. In Yong Zhao's *World Class Learners*, the author discusses the fact that schools do not encourage creativity but instead "prepare good employees" (2012, p. 15). He advocates that education should never suppress curiosity and imagination. Taking that a step further, I would argue that schools should create opportunities to foster curious minds and pursue imagination, both in their students and teachers.

> Schools should create opportunities to foster curious minds and pursue imagination, both in its students and teachers.

Gregg Behr, executive director of The Grable Foundation, recently stated, "Today, new pioneers, gamers, roboticists, technologists, and designers are working alongside educators in and out of schools to inspire and provoke creativity and curiosity among children and youth in the region" (Coon, 2012). The freedom and flexibility to explore STEAM and making can be a challenge within a standards-based, accountability-driven educational system. It is a challenge that schools are taking along with community partners, libraries, parents, and corporations, positioning STEAM Making as a viable solution for positive educational change. This change is echoed by Sir Ken Robinson, ultimate supporter of creativity and innovation in schools.

In his 2006 TED Talk, Robinson implored educators to accept this changing paradigm and begin thinking about a new approach to teaching. His talk attained close to thirty-two million views on YouTube. He asserted that schools kill creativity and spoke about the uncertainty of the future. We know now that STEAM and the Maker Movement have forged ahead as a means to develop creativity and innovation in our students. Are you ready to accept this change and embrace the opportunities that come with STEAM Making in your classroom?

TRY IT CHECKLIST

Still not convinced that this idea is worth trying? If you can check off more than one thing on the checklist, then STEAM Making will bring value to your classroom.

Try It Checklist

I want my students to be able to

- ☐ Think critically about a topic, question, or problem
- ☐ Analyze those topics, questions, or problems
- ☐ Research information
- ☐ Direct their own learning
- ☐ Work successfully on a team
- ☐ Possess oral and written communication skills
- ☐ Work independently to complete a task
- ☐ Explain concepts thoroughly
- ☐ Apply learning to the real world
- ☐ Serve in leadership roles

In what ways do I promote and honor both left-brain and right-brain thinking in my teaching?

_____

_____

_____

_____

_____

_____

_____

How might STEAM and making fit into the learning happening in my classroom/school?

_____

_____

_____

_____

_____

_____

What do I need to integrate my subject area/classroom/content with others to ensure that students are breaking out of the silos and engaging in meaningful learning in science, technology, engineering, art, and math?

_____

_____

_____

_____

_____

_____

CHAPTER 2

CHaNge

Change is the law of life and those who look only to the past or present are certain to miss the future.

—John F. Kennedy

In a 2014 *Newsweek* article, Louise Stewart stated that, "Ten years from now, primary and secondary education may look more like a scene from Tim Allen's *The Santa Clause* than Ben Stein's economics class in *Ferris Bueller's Day Off*." While I couldn't agree more, I think we need to anticipate this change occurring a lot sooner than the ten-year mark suggested by Stewart. Classrooms across the country are already turning into studios, workshops, and makerspaces.

As STEAM and making become more prominent in K–12 schools, educators will be faced with change: change of practice, change of the physical learning space, change of school curriculum, change of mindset. Unfortunately, adapting to change is not always easy. I don't claim that these changes have been easy for schools already engaged in STEAM Making, which is why common obstacles and barriers will be addressed throughout the upcoming chapters.

Schools that are successfully implementing STEAM Making have support. Some believe that initiatives cannot be successful without involvement from visionary leaders. Backing from "higher ups" is huge, but garnering support isn't always easy. Others believe that grassroots efforts that start at the classroom level grow into successful programs. How can we engage *all* stakeholders to ensure that STEAM and the Maker Movement receive the support needed to continue to grow?

DISTRICT LEADERSHIP

Superintendents and school boards may not be familiar with STEAM and making. Sharing articles, websites, and books (like this one) may help district leaders see the relevance in this type of teaching and learning. Appendix F features a list of websites that support STEAM and making.

For many school boards and superintendents, often it all comes down to money. There are low-cost ways to start programs in STEAM Making without lots of technology, fancy machinery, or extra staff. Using everyday household items and recyclable materials are a good start. A few cans of paint can transform a learning space with a splash of color. This might happen in one classroom and spread to multiple rooms. It might begin as a lunchtime activity or during an after-school program.

It is important to start the conversations around STEAM and making with district leadership. Whether you are talking about a small change or a large-scale one, they will need to be in the loop. These all-important stakeholders should also hear about community partnerships and grants that are available to schools implementing these initiatives. Chapter 6 will focus on establishing community and corporate partners to leverage your programs forward. Chapter 7 will address ways to generate funds including grants.

What do superintendents think about when it comes to new initiatives? Regarding transformation in his district, Elizabeth Forward superintendent Dr. Bart Rocco said during a school tour, "It has completely changed the culture of our school and community." With his vision for change and enthusiastic leadership style, Rocco has put his district on the map. Elizabeth Forward School District has educators from across the globe visiting its schools to see their innovative learning spaces and unique programs. (Read more about them in Chapter 5.) Superintendent Amy Burch talks about creativity and innovation from her perspective as a newly appointed superintendent (see sidebar on the next page).

Support at the district level is important with any new initiative, but it is often a more local effort that moves STEAM and making in the right direction. Building level leadership can promote and support teaching and learning. Leadership on the part of the principal is a key component to successful change.

PRINCIPAL LEADERSHIP

When principals take the lead, initiatives in STEAM and making can really take off! Principal leadership that includes permission to try new things and support to improve instructional practices are evident in the school stories that will be shared in later chapters. The leaders described in this book are innovative risk takers with big ideas and the commitment to quality learning for young people. Principals and other building leaders can do several things to support creativity and innovation in their schools. Support can be shown through four major strands:

- Time
- Money
- Resources
- Professional development

Dr. Amy Burch, superintendent of the Brentwood Borough School District, embraces new initiatives, especially those that will enhance the educational experience for her students. Her district started considering STEAM programming in 2013. Her advice to districts and leaders falls into three steps:

- Do your own research
- Look for application
- Explore potential resources

She shares four guiding questions:

- What are we already doing that fits?
- Where do we want to go as a district?
- What value will students walk away with?
- How can the district measure success?

When she explored these questions for herself, she found that STEAM and making experiences were lacking in her district. Through informal research, she knew that employers were looking for qualities in young people that could be fostered through new programming. Her leadership team explored local funding and has now developed programs at the elementary, middle, and high school levels.

Most decisions made in education take these components into consideration. Principals are often the ones to find the money, carve out the time, and plan the professional development. These are needed when any change is taking place in a school, but support also means that the principal or leader needs to be a "change maker."

CHANGE MAKERS

Change makers provide ongoing encouragement and validation during a change. Change makers dig into the initiative and aren't afraid to "get their hands dirty." In the context of STEAM and making, school leaders are getting their hands dirty (often literally) as they tinker with tools, explore with clay, or build a model. When a leader models the expectation, then others are more apt to do the same.

At a recent in-service, the teachers in my school attended an introductory session on design thinking. (The d.school at Stanford University has done a lot to push this idea into the hands of educators. Their website (**http://dschool.stanford.edu**) is a great resource.) Our first attempt at design thinking was merely a way for teachers to think about problems and come up with creative solutions. Teams worked together in a hands-on way, developing physical models. Teams used cardboard, plastic bottles, buttons, wire, paper, and other odds and ends to construct their project. I knew that if I wanted my teachers to step out of their comfort zones and start making, then as the principal, I needed to be there grappling alongside of them. Even more meaningful, they were able to see my struggle with generating ideas and building something . . . the same struggle students go through when trying something new and open ended. Principals can't just be visible at an in-service training or professional development sessions; they need to be engaged, active participants.

d.school

PARENTS AND COMMUNITY

Parents and community members are an important part of any school program. Getting parents "on board" can be achieved in a number of ways. STEAM and making are likely new ideas for parents and community members. As a school leader or classroom teacher, it will be important to share this change with them. One powerful way is to let them experience for themselves. When we initiated our STEAM studio at Crafton Elementary, we had an open house from 3 to 8 pm. We welcomed parents, grandparents, siblings, and community members in to tinker and play. Our students served as the tour guides, showing materials to our guests and demonstrating some of their projects. Parents sat with preschoolers trying out Rokenbok blocks and weaving boards. The vibe in the studio was one of excitement and interest; everyone wanted to see and do everything. This initial engagement helped to pave the way for future programs. We also put a lot of information out to parents through school newsletters, websites, and community magazines, sharing pictures and stories of the cool things happening in our school. For a lot of parents, that is enough, but others may not be sold on this new approach. Leery parents may have questions:

- Why are STEAM and making important?
- What will my child be doing/making?
- What does that look like?
- Will they have homework?
- Will this be graded?

- What safety precautions are in place?
- And many more . . .

Parents can also get involved by sharing their expertise in school. Parents can be guest speakers, talking with students about their careers. We've had parents come in and talk about their work as civil engineers, landscape architects, X-ray technicians, and patent attorneys. We've had other parents come in and talk about their passions. Parents have spoken about their love of rebuilding motorcycles, designing websites, and sewing. There are so many skills that your parents and community can contribute. When it comes to STEAM and making, reach out and invite people in! You never know who has something to offer that can potentially improve your program.

Having support from the top and from parents and community are critical, but teachers have to be active in the change process if any initiative is going to stick. While some teachers may be reluctant, many are leading the change

The Reluctant Teacher

With every new initiative, there are teachers who jump right on board. There are other teachers who are willing to try but need a little assistance. There are also a few who dig in their heels and say, "This too shall pass."

Mrs. Morris was not the kind of teacher who wanted to make waves. She did things the way she had always done them, and that was just fine with her. She saw no need to add anything new to the curriculum, especially something that required teachers to hand over control to the students. The idea of STEAM and making took her out of her comfort zone.

So, how did she get to be the teacher designing contraptions and allowing students to design contraptions and drop eggs off of balconies?

Change takes time. Mrs. Morris was like many teachers in that she needed to see that things worked before she jumped right in. As her colleagues experimented with making, she tiptoed in, testing the waters. She tried a few activities that were comfortable, first in small groups, as opposed to in her class of 25. She tried some team teaching, working with a parent or instructional aide in the room. Some hands-on professional development sessions with experts also helped to nudge her along. With constant encouragement from the principal, Mrs. Morris began to take small steps toward including more hands-on opportunities in her class and collaborating with other teachers engaging in STEAM and making. She found some great children's literature to accompany some design challenges and pretty soon she was off and running.

for STEAM and making in schools. You'll read about some of their efforts in later chapters.

CHANGE FOR TEACHERS

Change is hard. No one likes it, right? And now education is changing things. Again. Teachers have seen changes come and go. They are used to the cycle of initiatives that come back around every so many years. Could STEAM and making be one of those fads? Maybe. But it's one that is gaining momentum and should be considered as a valuable shift in education.

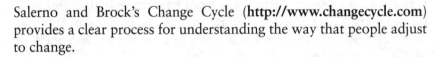

Responding to change is different for anyone, but there are several stages to consider.

Change Cycle

Salerno and Brock's Change Cycle (**http://www.changecycle.com**) provides a clear process for understanding the way that people adjust to change.

- **Loss.** At the beginning of any change, you feel cautious (and rightfully so). You are moving away from the known to the unknown. Letting go of "the way things have always been" is difficult but possible.

- **Doubt.** Teachers can be resistant to change and feel skeptical about what is to come. It is OK to question new changes, but when you see the response from students engaged in STEAM and making, doubt will turn to hope and possibility.

- **Discomfort.** Change is not comfortable. We need to make adjustments to our practice, but when teachers feel anxious they may become unproductive. With leadership and support, teachers can get involved in STEAM and making and gain more comfort in using these as instructional strategies.

- **Discovery.** This is when the momentum can really shift. Upon uncovering the potential benefits of the change, teachers begin to feel energized and think in resourceful ways.

- **Understanding.** When teacher confidence builds, teachers become productive. This is when the movers and shakers embrace the change and run with it, expanding programs, taking risks, and innovating.

- **Integration.** Getting here takes time, but full integration of the new change will happen. Teachers will feel satisfied with their progress and can focus their thoughts on moving forward.

In schools where STEAM and making are occurring, teachers are moving through various stages at any given point in time. Support from peers and school leaders is critical. Regional networks are also a great way to garner support from others going through the change. (The Remake Learning

Network in Pittsburgh will be discussed in Chapter 6). Social media is another great way to build a teacher support network. Facebook, Pinterest, and Twitter are all great to connect with others and share ideas.

Some Change Makers Across the Country Active in STEAM and Making	
@DianaLRedina	@MakerSylvia
@KristinZiemke	@IntoOutside
@NMHS_lms	@sciteach212
@Teach21Tech	@ms_deljuidice
@MAKESHOP	@ZeinaChalich
@DrToddKeruskin	@kerszi
@garystager	@geekyteach
@smartinez	@ShaneAbell

SHALER AREA ELEMENTARY: CHANGES SPACES

Most elementary school classrooms are basically the same: square or rectangular in shape, a few windows (if you're lucky), neutral colored walls, a board (chalk or white), and some bulletin boards. Every teacher does what she can to brighten up rooms with colorful displays, posters, and maybe a bright rug. Sound accurate? Some schools are transforming classrooms beyond recognition. These efforts are tied to a common goal to engage children in STEAM Maker learning.

Imagine taking an average space, like the one described above, and creating a phenomenal learning space. Shaler Area Elementary School changed one room in the school and ended up changing the school culture along with it!

Picture a large, darkened room, lit only by the controls on the dashboard of a spaceship. Touchscreens at every station provide up-to-date information to the teams trying to achieve a mission. Some team members are sharing ideas and calling out information from their captain's chairs. You wouldn't believe that this is a look into an elementary school classroom.

The school has transformed one of its classrooms into a dream flight simulator (**http://dreamflightadventures.com**). This space is now the bridge of a space ship called the "IKS Titan." This interactive

Dream Flight Adventures

learning environment teaches students teamwork, critical thinking, problem solving, and effective communication, while integrating rigorous content. Opened in 2013, this innovative addition has increased interest and enthusiasm in STEAM learning for the 1,000 students in Grades 4 through 6. Groups of students are able to enter into the simulator, work together to operate it, and use it to go on a wide variety of educational adventures.

Dream Flight Missions

Mission: Succession has students exploring monarchies, democracy, and republics, nuclear isotopes and radioactive decay, marine biology, and checks and balances in the U.S. government.

Curriculum Connection: Written reflection—How do history and tradition influence the way governments are established?

Mission: Pandemic integrates anatomy and physiology as students study immune, circulatory, and lymphatic systems. Using the scientific method, they analyze viruses and viral reproduction and disease resistance.

Curriculum Connection: Class debate—Should actions be taken to maintain genetic diversity?

Mission: Contaminant considers the interconnectedness of living things while investigating aquatic ecosystems and food chains. Students examine acidity, alkalinity, and water purification.

Curriculum Connection: Written reflection—What responsibilities do community stakeholders have when it comes to protecting the environment?

Inside the simulator, students travel to space, explore under the sea, enter the human body, and go back in time. Each member of the crew has a role in the completion of the ship's mission. Students study topics for each mission, ensuring that they understand the content before participating in the hands-on, minds-on experience. "Since missions are set up much like video games, kids are thoroughly engaged. They want to try again. They want to learn to do it better," explains assistant superintendent Kara Eckert (personal communication, January 19, 2015). It was her vision, with urging from Dream Flight's Gary Gardiner to create this unconventional learning space.

The IKS missions merge content from a variety of topics: history, literature, and biology. The students delve into social and ethical issues that require them to think beyond general course content. Missions are challenging for students, as the teachers step back and serve as facilitators rather than instructors, requiring decision making and problem solving on the part of the students.

IKS Titan

Once the simulator was unveiled to students, adults wanted to participate too. Events were held for teachers, parents, and other local educators to experience the missions. Clearly, this is a one-of-a-kind project that embraces the integration of science, technology, engineering, art, and mathematics. "This space is special . . . everyone has a role here. We have a student that doesn't talk, but she performs here," said Eckert (personal communication, January 19, 2015).

More and more large-scale simulators like this one are being installed in schools across the country. Transforming a classroom into a simulator requires commitment on the part of the school district. Dream Flight Adventures is looking for more schools to get involved. The organization also works with districts to secure the funds needed to build this unique learning tool.

IKS Titan Dashboard

Obstacles

At first, the actual construction of the simulator seemed to be the greatest challenge. Transforming a classroom into this innovative space required a lot of work. Unique materials were brought in to give the simulator the "WOW" factor. Eckert gives all the credit to the custodial and maintenance staff. They even found an old ship door to be installed in the simulator! With help from district staff, including teachers, custodians, and administrators, the simulator was completed in about four months.

"We are using this as a springboard for other projects. We recognize that it can't be a one-shot wonder" (Kara Eckert, personal communication, January 19, 2015). As the Shaler Area looks to expand its programming, staff members continue to pursue outside funding; they are hoping to get a National Science Foundation grant to create ten units of instruction to be developed with Dream Flight and other area districts that are in the process of designing and installing similar spaces.

Growing Ideas

The next endeavor for Shaler staff and students is the creation of a STEAM summer camp. The weeklong camp will allow students to choose four specialized sessions. In one session, participants will explore the world of robotics and teamwork by learning to design and build using the Lego Mindstorms program. Another session integrates math and art, as students explore plane geometry and apply these concepts to the creation of an optical illusion. Students will engage in a bridge-building project in another camp offering. The district plans to utilize community resources, like the local science center, to facilitate workshops on the science of sports. The district also connected with a local theater group to facilitate a class on integrating movement, creativity, and dance.

Lego

Other departments are growing STEAM ideas within their programs as well. Following a successful after-school club he piloted, the tech teacher overhauled his curriculum to include a nine-week rotation of Lego Mindstorms (**http://www.lego.com/en-us/mindstorms/?domainredir=mindstorms.lego.com**). Students have the opportunity to build and program robots that walk, talk, and think. Teams navigate their robots through various obstacles and have even taken their robots to regional competitions. The computer lab now has a dedicated space for robotics materials as well as a table where students can test out their creations.

After receiving a grant, the music room has also transformed into a colorful space that includes brightly colored wall panels and storage units, a ballet bar, a music studio, and a lounge area. When the students head to music class, they might be composing music on the iPads using the GarageBand app (**https://www.apple.com/ios/garageband**). Students can write, remix, and release their own music using the tool. Embracing the integration of subjects, students also engage in reading strategies in music class, using sticky notes to improve comprehension while reading music.

GarageBand

Robotics Table

Shaler Area School District has also created a STEAM Advisory Council. The goal of this group is to create more programming at the secondary level. The council is also exploring different pathways to STEAM careers. The idea of digital badging is also a topic of interest for the group. (Badging will be discussed in the next chapter.)

This innovative school district changed the idea of what a classroom could look like. They transformed a learning space and developed programs that supported student interest while embracing unique technologies. As they continue to grow new ideas for STEAM learning, the district will undoubtedly go through more changes, but it is this growth that will prepare them for the changing future.

Lesson: Can you make that?

Goal: Explore recyclable materials and create an original design. Write the steps needed to make it and see if your partner can re-create it.

Timeframe: Can be done as a brief ice breaker within 30 minutes or explored more elaborately over several class periods.

Possible Materials:

fabric	yarn
beads	cardboard
plastic bottles	glue
wire	popsicle sticks

Procedures: Each partner should gather materials to craft an original creation. (For a back-to-school spin, it could be something that describes them to their classmates. During the school year, the item could be something that connects to a story read in class. At the end of the year, it might be a preview to what they are looking forward to doing over the summer.) Time should be allotted for all students to build on their own without viewing their partner's. Each individual writes the steps to re-create the piece. The partners reunite and attempt to follow the directions that their partner has provided using the same materials. Partnerships should share their creations with the group and receive feedback on their work.

Reflection: Did you come up with similar creations? Students should reflect on the clarity of their directions and identify things that they might have included in an effort to improve communication in the future.

CHILDREN'S MUSEUM OF PITTSBURGH: LEADING THE ACTION

The Children's Museum of Pittsburgh is changing what museums are all about! This is not a museum to walk around and gaze at galleries, although there is a lot to look at. There are no "do not touch" signs, except the one

My Son Caden, Building in the MAKESHOP®

next to a paint rack where kids leave their paintings to dry. This is an active place, like no other you've visited. But beyond the active learning exhibits like a water room, climbing areas, clay table, screen printing, slides, and trains, the museum boasts the MAKESHOP®. It is an exciting spot—a makerspace for children and families, at the heart of the museum where you can find dads and daughters working in the woodshop, neighbors learning to weave, or preschoolers creating a marble run out of PVC pipes. The MAKESHOP® is a space that is different each time you visit. "Teaching artists" facilitate the space and engage visitors in the process of making and helping them to translate their ideas into tangible products (Lisa Brahms, personal communication, February 5, 2015). Sometimes kids want to learn about circuits or building a car. Others want to learn how to sew a pillow for a doll or construct a doghouse.

In Pittsburgh, the children's museum is one of the major players leading the Maker Movement. The museum is a part of an interconnected network of schools, community groups, researchers, and organizations working together to build meaningful learning for young people in both formal and informal settings. During a conversation with Children's Museum of Pittsburgh's Samantha Ellwood, manager of educational programs, and Lisa Brahms, director of learning and research, we discussed what it is that makes STEAM and making important. They spoke about the way that it gets teachers to think differently, "to be more comfortable with the uncomfortable," Samantha explained. Lisa expressed the need for harnessing the experiences in making that kids and families are having in the museum and getting this out into the schools. She went on to say, "Things like choice, innovation, and imaginative thinking didn't really happen before." With schools across the country now embracing this philosophy, many organizations are interested in the connection between STEAM and making. Lisa defined this uniquely, "There's a lot more that goes into making—it's like an on-ramp to STEAM." Samantha talks about this a little differently, "For many, the *A* was an afterthought. We believe that the *A* needs to shine through!"

Tinkering at the MAKESHOP®

The museum offers the chance for visitors to make choices based on their interests.

Makers can explore a variety of pathways or focus on one more deeply. This is happening in schools as well. Since the museum works with many schools in various capacities, they shared an example of one local school that is basing everything on student interest. The students were interested in paper airplanes, so the teachers did a whole unit on paper airplanes. Then the making expanded to parachutes, kites, and gliders, culminating in a design challenge. Rather than the educators determining the path, student voice is a part of the lesson plan.

Samantha and Lisa's advice for those ready to jump into STEAM and making includes the following:

1. Have an open mind.

2. Educators should approach making as learners and makers first—dive into the process and get your hands dirty.

3. Invest in people, their passions, and expertise over stuff (equipment and supplies).

The MAKESHOP® is changing informal learning in Pittsburgh. In 2013, a group of traditional and unconventional educators came together through the leadership of the Children's Museum of Pittsburgh to embark on a new project—the Mobile MAKESHOP®. This advisory group was selected from applicants around the Pittsburgh area, some even coming from across West Virginia. Teachers, assistant superintendents, museum staff, community librarians, and faculty from higher education met over the course of the year to share ideas about making in schools and communities. The group discussed the potential benefits and challenges of taking the idea of the MAKESHOP®, a permanent museum exhibit, and transferring that experi-

ence outside the museum walls. Within the advisory committee, topics for discussion included the changing role for teachers and librarians, the emphasis on process not product, and questions about funding and sustainability.

At the end of that year, five locations were selected to be Mobile MAKESHOP® sites. You will hear about their individual experiences throughout this book. Each took a different approach to making based on their time, space, and organization, but each resulted in permanent change to the culture and practice—thanks to the leadership and support from The Pittsburgh Children's Museum.

Messing With Clay at the MAKESHOP®

THE ROLE OF FACILITATOR: CHANGING HOW WE TALK TO KIDS

Taking on the role of a facilitator is different from being the teacher. A facilitator guides but rarely tells. A facilitator questions and nudges but doesn't lead. A facilitator recognizes that someone else in the room might have more knowledge than he does. (This is a tough one for teachers.) Shifting from lecture and direct instruction toward facilitation can be a challenge.

Think about current math and science instruction. We teach students how to solve the problem or set up the experiment. We often tell them the steps, give them the processes, and show them the way. We model what we expect of them. We make them practice the steps over and over again. We reteach.

What if the teacher didn't provide a method or walk students through every step? What if we posed broad questions and left students to learn and discover in their own way? What if we regularly engaged our students in open-ended design challenges and making experiences and instead of directing their learning, we stepped back and observed? How might thinking and learning change in response? Table 2.1 provides sample questions to facilitate learning experiences.

The questions in Table 2.1 can help to facilitate experiences like making but can really be used in many learning opportunities. Often, the way we ask a question changes the response. Consider asking a student the following questions:

> Did you encounter any problems while you were building your rocket?

> Tell me about some challenges you had during the building process.

A student could easily respond to a yes or no question without elaborating on his or her learning. Asking students to describe or tell you about something allows the learner to be in charge and take responsibility for the design process. This also gives the teacher the chance to step back and hear from the student. As the student explains, the teacher also gains a better understanding of what the student knows and understands about the concepts.

The role of facilitator can be a challenging one for teachers. Developing a strong repertoire of open-ended questions is an important step toward effective STEAM Making instruction. With strong leadership, the teachers at Avonworth Elementary are taking on the role of facilitator as their school experiments with the Maker Movement.

AVONWORTH ELEMENTARY: CHANGING PRACTICES

For principal Scott Miller, "it's all about integrated experiences." He described the problem that he saw in education in a meeting on January 23, 2015: "Everything was happening in isolation and there was no transfer."

TABLE 2.1 Questions to Facilitate Learning Experiences

INITIAL
What are you working on?
What's your plan?
What background knowledge do you have, and how will it help to facilitate this process?
Why did you choose these particular materials?
Did you consider any other designs?
What purpose does it serve?

DEVELOPMENTAL
Can you make a sketch or a model to help you design your _____?
What is your next step?
Is there another way to solve that problem?
How could we try to _____?
What were you thinking when you _____?
How might you accomplish your goal?
How would the outcome be different if you chose _____ instead of _____ material?
Did you consider proportions of measurements in your model?
How are you contributing to the group?
What is your role?

REFLECTIVE
What obstacles did you encounter?
What would you change or do differently next time?
What advice would you give to others about making/using _____?
Is your end result what you expected?
How did your original design change with the end product?
Are there any other materials you wish you had?

Faced with this problem, like many school leaders, he decided to take action and make a change in his school. With an opportunity to partner with the Pittsburgh Children's Museum, Scott jumped at the chance to get involved.

Through a unique partnership, Avonworth Elementary School serves as a Mobile MAKESHOP® site. This is one of five sites in the Western Pennsylvania region to take the ideas of making out into the community. (The other sites include another elementary school, a library, a community center, and a university.) The concept of making was introduced to teachers through a kick-off event in the fall of 2013. The session provided staff with an overview of the elements of making, the design process, and the possibilities for integration into the curriculum. Most importantly, the sessions engaged them in hands-on experiences and design challenges.

Avonworth Makers

In an effort to promote this instructional shift, museum staff brought in tools, materials, and storage items to establish an environment conducive to making. One day each week a skilled teaching artist worked directly with elementary school teachers and students engaging in making activities. The teaching artist facilitated a variety of experiences for children and adults in woodworking, circuitry, sewing, building and design, and digital animation, with the goal of bringing museum learning into schools.

START SMALL, ENGAGE ALL

Miller initially decided that the teaching artist would focus his work with the school's youngest learners in kindergarten. The teaching artist pushed into each of six classrooms and provided a 45-minute lesson in one area of making each week. The classroom-based sessions encouraged hands-on learning with raw materials in order to facilitate an interactive learning experience. Students were given the opportunity to use real tools: hammers, screwdrivers, and sewing needles. The teaching artist served as a facilitator, as opposed to providing direct instruction, as some of the teachers were used to. He used open-ended questions, pushing both the teacher and the students to think a little more.

Change Maker Chat: Developing the Maker Mindset

"We started slow and let things grow organically," said Miller. He provided some initial professional development so that teachers could begin to understand the principles of practice. "I think it's really important to experience it yourself!" He invited teachers to Maker Boot Camp hosted at the Children's Museum of Pittsburgh each summer. This four-day experience, offered annually, immerses teachers in hands-on learning.

He shared articles with faculty and staff, but ultimately, he allowed teachers to discover making on their own and find ways to integrate it into their work in meaningful ways that worked for them. His approach followed these steps:

- Provide learning opportunities
- Give support
- Repeat

Principal leadership was a key component to successful implementation. The principal provided ongoing coaching and professional development to teachers. He allotted time for team planning and collaboration, which helped teachers to begin to shift their practice. Professional development sessions with Children's Museum of Pittsburgh staff underscored the value of the making experience. Teachers received coaching from the teaching artist but also attended a mini boot camp at the Museum tailored to the needs of the school. Museum staff provided a crash course in sewing, woodworking, and Scratch. (The easy-to-use, free digital animation program is available on MIT's website, **https://scratch .mit.edu.**)

Scratch

Teachers at every grade level were able to build skills and envision ways they could connect making to their existing curriculum. Miller reminded teachers, "You never know what direction the child's going to go with their learning." With this in mind, the faculty moved away from more traditional approaches to teaching and embraced a mindset of being more open-ended in the way they designed lessons and in the way they interacted with students.

As the partnership with the museum evolved, the teachers began to design centers for use in their room as part of their classroom instruction. Soon, the concept of classroom centers evolved from an instructional strategy to a cultural focus; it became the norm in every classroom. Teachers at all grade levels embraced this philosophy, not just those in the primary grades. Teachers adopted concepts of making into daily practice, allowing the students to explore elements of design regularly. With success at the classroom level, Miller wanted to expand this throughout the school and community.

Parent involvement allowed families to see this new concept in action. Not only did parents see the enthusiasm from their children, they also engaged in new learning themselves. As a culmination of the first year of this project, a special celebration was held at the children's museum. The free event helped to promote the making culture while attendees explored the museum's MAKESHOP® and other exhibits.

One major component to the success of the makerspace at Avonworth was the involvement of the parents. "The community was talking about it," said Miller. An already active PTA wanted to know more and sought out information from the school. What do we need to know about this? How can we use it? Miller brought parents in and talked to them about his vision. He got parents excited, which allowed the enthusiasm to grow. He shared knowledge and resources with parents and teachers, empowering them to drive the initiative forward. The parents even took on the responsibility of stocking the school's makerspace. They sought out donations and collected materials.

This school was fortunate to get a start with some tools and a cart from the MAKESHOP®, but it was able to successfully sustain its work into Year 2 with the help of its PTA. This group of active parents leads activities, cleans

TABLE 2.2 Sample Parent Flier

DONATIONS NEEDED!	
KINDERGARTEN HOMEROOMS	
Room 101	Water and other drink bottle caps
Room 103	Buttons
Room 104	Ping pong balls
Room 105	Clothes pins and large binder clips
Room 110	Popsicle sticks
Room 112	Empty cereal boxes
FIRST-GRADE HOMEROOMS	
Room 202	Cardboard boxes
Room 203	Thread needles
Room 204	Wood scraps
Room 207	Packing supplies (bubble wrap, packing peanuts)
Room 208	Fabric
Room 210	Egg cartons
SECOND-GRADE HOMEROOMS	
Room 306	Pipe cleaners, poms-poms, or other craft items
Room 307	Foam trays
Room 308	Metal hangers
Room 309	Yarn and string
Room 311	Toilet paper/towel rolls
Room 312	Broken toys

up in the makerspace, and supports the school with donations. Each homeroom is now responsible for stocking an item or two in the school's makerspace. Collecting egg cartons, bottle caps, fabric, and cardboard are all supplies that allow the students to keep their creations going. Table 2.2 is an example of a flier that went home to families so that each class could be responsible for a few specific items in the school's makerspace.

Obstacles

"There are so many competing messages about time in education" (Scott Miller, personal communication, January 23, 2015). School leaders need to set aside time for interventions, testing, preparing for the tests, more interventions, and more tests. But, when is there time set aside for students to develop creativity and engage in collaborative projects? "For us, it wasn't about the acronym, STEM or STEAM. It's about how you can create a meaningful experience for kids," explained Miller.

Growing Ideas

Principal Miller would like to expand programming within his school and across the district. He is also exploring partnerships with other schools committed to integrating making into their classes. He is planning school visits with other innovative schools in the area as well as the possibility of sharing professional development ideas and costs as a way to build a making network of schools.

Miller is partnering with other schools to try and get some funding to develop a mentoring program. The idea is for schools that have already embraced the Maker Movement to partner with another school that wants to get started. Schools with developed programs could serve as mentors, providing guidance and sharing ideas. The partner schools could share professional development and even resources.

THE CHALLENGER LEARNING CENTER AT WHEELING JESUIT UNIVERSITY

The Challenger Learning Center at Wheeling Jesuit (**http://clc.cet .edu/?/home**) is changing what it means to go on a field trip. This educational center in Wheeling, West Virginia, is one of forty centers around the country that serve formal and informal educators, undergraduate and graduate students, and students in K–12 schools. Schools in Ohio, Pennsylvania, and West Virginia have been accessing this center for the last twenty years.

Challenger Learning Center

Inspired by the January 28, 1986, Challenger disaster, family members of the crew collaborated to develop a place where an interest in science and engineering could be sparked through space missions. Conducting experiments, using specialized equipment and problem solving, students (and teachers) are able to immerse themselves in space exploration. The Challenger Learning Center at Wheeling Jesuit (CLC@ WJ) provides a variety of opportunities to support student learning in STEAM.

Challenger Pre-Mission

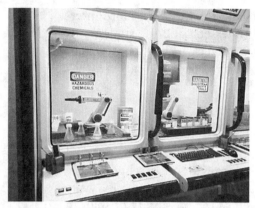

Challenger Simulator Tasks

The center hosts visits on campus that engage guests in a space simulation. Students and teachers become pilots, medics, and researchers, as they visit the moon, rendezvous with a comet, or take a voyage to Mars.

The trip to Wheeling is taken by thousands of students each year, but the center understands that everyone can't participate on site. (It is several hundred dollars for a class to visit, in addition to lunch and transportation.) CLC@WJ also offers distance-learning options called e-Missions. These missions are live and conducted via videoconference. Student teams interact with "mission control" to avert weather disasters, evacuate islands, and provide supplies to satellites as the scenario unfolds and conditions change. Throughout the mission, new data is provided to student teams; as they analyze it, they must make recommendations to the flight director at mission control. Missions are fast paced and provide a real glimpse into the work of astronauts, scientists, and engineers that work with NASA.

Challenger Mission Control

Schools that have connected with the CLC@WJ build this experience into their curriculum. Teachers have linked content in math and science to the work that students will do during their mission. Students learn about geography, geology, astronomy, and physics prior to the mission. They have to be comfortable using technology as they upload data, synthesize information, and communicate with others. The "takeaway" for students is really powerful. When asked what they thought about the experience, one sixth grader responded, "That was the coolest thing I've ever done!"

STEAM-y in nature, some schools are adding a making component to their missions as well. Crafton Elementary builds in a graphic design component to the mission. Much like NASA creates a patch for each mission, students design a T-shirt for everyone to wear on mission day. All designs are considered and scored by students, faculty, and staff before the winning design is chosen. The designs from each year, over the course of the last twenty, are framed and proudly hung in the school's sixth-grade wing.

SUMMARY

Education is changing, both in formal and informal settings. Innovative learning like what is taking place in Shaler Area and Avonworth are serving as outstanding examples of STEAM and making programs. The collaborative work of the Pittsburgh Children's Museum supports formal educators as they implement new initiatives in their schools. STEAM and making combined allow us to truly innovate. Schools and organizations embracing these concepts are proving that change is possible.

EXPANDING YOUR THINKING

Brainstorm a list of spaces in your school that need a makeover. How might they be reconfigured and serve as a STEAM Maker space?

_____

_____

_____

_____

_____

_____

In what ways can you enlist parents or engage your community to stock your learning space?

_____

_____

_____

_____

_____

_____

_____

How might you begin to connect STEAM Making activities to existing learning goals, units, or lesson plans?

_____

_____

_____

_____

_____

_____

_____

CHAPTER 3

FAiL

Failure is instructive. The person, who really thinks, learns quite as much from his failures as from his successes.

—John Dewey

One Saturday morning, I sat watching my almost three-year-old son as he tinkered with some blocks, cardboard boxes, and toy cars. With a very serious look on his face, he was clearly designing something important. (He was constructing a multilevel garage to house all of his toy cars.) His brows furrowed. He took pieces apart. At one point, he slammed down his fists and exhaled a loud "ugh!" He moved around, grabbed a different block and tried again. While his multilevel car garage continued to grow and change, he encountered challenges. Things didn't work. He got frustrated, but yet he persevered. I watched as he teetered back and forth between failure and success. When he got to the point where he was satisfied, the look of pride was astounding. He had conquered his challenge. "Look Mama, I did it!"

We have all felt failure of one kind or another: a failing grade, not getting the job, not making a relationship work. As adults, we have failed at lots of things over the course of our lives, and failure did not feel good. How you respond to failure is what sets you apart from others. Do your failures set you back and cause you to withdraw? Or do you use them as fuel to move forward? If you haven't experienced a lot of failures, persevering may be a challenge. When we think about failures, this can happen with students and teachers. For teachers, taking risks means there is a possibility of failure. What if I try this and it doesn't work? What if others see me as a failure? Our students wonder those things too! Traditional schooling isn't set up for taking risks and accepting failures. We teach the content until we are sure our students understand it, then we test them to see if they have mastered it. Engaging in STEAM and making means that both teachers and students will get a little more comfortable with failure.

Being innovative in the classroom is risky. It means that things will not go right the first time and probably not the second. Innovation means that you must put down the manual, the curriculum guide, and the chalk, and think outside the box. Your students already are! But moving outside of your comfort zone also means that things will be different, and that can be scary. One way to ease teachers and students into getting familiar with failure is to teach strategies and traits that allow them to better respond to challenges. For example, being persistent and thinking flexibly while creating are common behaviors in classrooms where STEAM Making is happening.

HABITS OF MIND

The Habits of Mind popularized by Costa and Kallick (2008) are being used in many schools where STEAM and making are central to student learning. Often referred to as "soft skills," these are life skills that embody what it means to be successful (see Table 3.1). As students design, redesign, collaborate, test, and share, they encounter problems. What do they do in this situation? It is often through this process and engaging learning opportunities that happen through STEAM and making that the Habits of Mind are needed.

Since many of these are developed internally and require active thinking, learners need modeling and regular practice with involved adults. In many schools, the Habits of Mind are explicitly taught. In others, the Habits are embedded in school character education programs. One particular school focuses on two Habits each month. They post them in classrooms and hallways and provide classroom instruction around the habits. During class meetings, teachers and students talk about what it looks and sounds like when people demonstrate the Habits. Learning opportunities in STEAM and making then allow students to practice and put the Habits into action.

Sir Ken Robinson talked about failure in his TED Talk, reminding educators that "kids will take a chance. They are not afraid of being wrong"; that is, until they come to school. He stresses that "if you're not prepared to be wrong, you'll never come up with anything original." He says, "We grow out

TABLE 3.1 Habits of Mind

Persisting	Striving for accuracy
Managing impulsivity	Questioning and posing problems
Listening and understanding with empathy	Thinking flexibly
Thinking about thinking	Applying past knowledge to new situations
Creating, imagining, innovating	Thinking and communicating with clarity
Finding humor	Gathering data through all senses
Remaining open to continuous learning	Taking responsible risks
Responding with wonderment and awe	Thinking interdependently

When we were getting our STEAM Studio up and running in the first year, I hosted competitions at lunch time to get students interested in what was going on in this "new room" in our school. One day, I showed students a YouTube video from a school not too far away from ours that showed elementary students building a Rube Goldberg device. The brief video showed students introducing what their device was supposed to do, followed by a series of failed attempts. My students were engaged as they watched a ping pong ball roll down a series of ramps and finally knock over a cup. I paired that with another video of high school students tackling a similar task but with a complex course that included dominoes, pulleys, a fan, and even a toaster! Their attempts numbered 148. In the final run, my students jumped up and cheered as they watched the success experienced by the students in the video. Their immediate response—can we do that?

Over the course of the next two days, the fifth- and sixth-grade students used cardboard tubes, marbles, string, tape, Popsicle sticks, and a sundry of other recycled materials to construct their own devices. We recorded our attempts, too. (Sixteen was our highest.) One carefully planned crew got theirs to work on the second try. Through this process, students struggled. Some got angry. Some left . . . only to return a few minutes later. While we hadn't focused a lot on the Habits of Mind up to this point, I observed so many traits in action through this project: persistence, striving for accuracy, thinking flexibly, and responding with wonderment and awe.

of creativity or we get educated out of it." We can't let that happen! There are plenty of ways that schools can develop creativity and innovation. STEAM and making are possible pathways to getting there.

In a recent conversation (January 2015) with Liz Parry, an engineer by trade and the coordinator for STEM partnership development in The Engineering Place at North Carolina State University, she asked an enormous question:

"How can we create an environment that says it's ok to fail?"

Liz is a certified trainer for Engineering is Elementary (EIE). The EIE program, established by the Museum of Science in Boston, facilitates the incorporation of engineering in the elementary school curriculum. Liz travels across the East Coast providing professional development to teachers. Her sessions provide teachers with hands-on engineering lessons—the same ones that their students do. This approach allows teachers to see the problem solving required to be successful. It also allows them to grapple with new concepts and deal with the malfunctions that their students will encounter.

WE NEED PROBLEM SOLVERS!

There comes a point when we need to ask ourselves what are we designing our lessons to accomplish? Mastery of content? Success on an assessment? The completion of the designated curriculum? While all of these may be part of the reality of teaching in a school system, there are many other outcomes that are desirable. "We need problem solvers!" Liz almost shouted during our meeting. She went on to describe how teachers are caught up in the vicious cycle of assessment and are bogged down with concerns about time.

"We don't have time to do this."

"We have a test on Friday."

"This doesn't fit in with my lesson plan."

Liz debunked these comments quickly. "The tests aren't the 'be all end all.' We need to be focusing on how to work with other people. Think about high school students. We can't teach them in isolation then expect that they'll synthesize it all the day after they graduate. So let's prepare them for that end goal." One way that we can prepare students for this is by helping them to become "technologically literate." She defined this literacy in three parts:

1. **Collaboration.** Students need multiple opportunities to work with other people. They need to work with other students, with teachers, and with experts in the field. They need to be able to interact in productive ways, communicating, respectfully disagreeing, and coming to consensus (or not). These are skills that will prepare them for life outside of school.

2. **Using Data.** Students need to feel comfortable with collecting, analyzing, and interpreting data. They also need ongoing opportunities to communicate and present data to others in a variety of formats. This is a process that students will use inside school and out.

3. **Fail and Recover.** We've talked about the importance of exposing students (and teachers) to failure, but the recovery phase is an integral part. Failure makes people feel helpless and reluctant to engage in risky tasks where failure can occur again. As educators, we need to reengage our students in these tasks and refocus them on their successes. Modeling failure and recovery for the class or sharing children's literature that highlights resilience are ways to rebuild this motivation with our students.

HOW SHOULD K–12 ENGINEERING BE TAUGHT?

In 2006, the National Academy of Engineering (NAE) and the National Research Council (NRC) convened a special committee to explore this question. The results, released in 2009, presented a vision for effective engineering education for young people, with an emphasis developing habits of mind for engineering. In my discussion with Liz Parry, she also identified the importance of the Engineering Habits of Mind. The six habits include the following:

- Systems thinking
- Creativity
- Optimism
- Collaboration
- Communication
- Attention to ethical considerations

I would argue that these habits of mind are applicable to all STEAM components, not just engineering. When combined, the habits allow young people to work together, investigate problems, and ponder solutions. Developing an ability to think flexibly helps students to prepare for life beyond school.

Systems Thinking

We need to demonstrate the interconnected nature of subject matter for our students and develop the understanding that STEAM subjects are interrelated. Systems thinking also requires critical thinking and the development of logical reasoning.

Creativity

Fostering the use of imagination in our students is critical for their success in the future. Creative thinking includes originality and flexibility (on the part of the students and teachers). Engaging students in the design process helps to develop creative and innovative thinking.

Optimism

As students engage in engineering or any STEAM-related learning, opportunities can be found in every challenge. It is important to foster a learning mindset in which students look for the possibilities in designing new things, using new technologies, and innovating for the future.

Collaboration

Classroom environments should be places that are supportive of student interactions and promote the knowledge and strengths of individuals but also the team. When students collaborate and participate, in-group discussions are facilitated and understanding is increased.

Communication

In a STEAM Making task, students are faced with challenges that often include defining a problem and communicating solutions. It is important for students to communicate their understandings, share ideas, and present their work to others.

Attention to Ethics

As students engage in design and engineering, they will need to consider factors outside of themselves. Accounting for safety, reliability, and aesthetics, as well as social and environmental impacts, may be new concepts for young engineers.

Engineering Resources

Teach Engineering Resources

Teach Engineering Resources K–12

http://www.teachengineering.org/whyk12engr.php

Engineering Habits of Mind in Science Classrooms

Engineering Habits of Mind in Science Classrooms

http://community.iisme.org/lessons/display .cfm?lessonid=1909&fileid=9295

National Academy of Engineering

National Academy of Engineering "K–12 Engineering Education"

https://www.nae.edu/Publications/Bridge/ 16145/16161.aspx

Children's Engineering Educators

Children's Engineering Educators

http://www.childrensengineering.com/ freeresources.htm

Virginia Children's Engineering Council

http://www.childrensengineering.org/technology/designbriefs.php

The Engineering Place

https://www.engr.ncsu.edu/theengineeringplace/educators/k8plans.php

Virginia Children's Engineering Council

The Engineering Place

Note: It may be helpful to cover other QR codes in this box with a sheet of paper to help focus your phone or tablet on a particular QR code.

The Engineering Habits of Mind are ones to consider as you develop a STEAM Maker program in your school. Some organizations adapt the habits and tailor them to their own needs. Some create their own big ideas that also speak to the core of the habits. During a visit to one innovative school, I came across a poster in a classroom that read (see sidebar on right):

I AM

- Visionary
- Courageous
- Collaborative
- Determined
- Reflective

These traits are ones that we want to develop in our students. STEAM and making are embedded with opportunities to develop the idea of an innovator's mindset. When **visionary** students are working on design challenges or engaging in making experiences, they can imagine things that don't exist yet and pursue them. **Courageous** thinkers stretch themselves to try new things and are willing to share their ideas. **Collaborative** learners develop their own perspectives but also find value in the perspectives of others. By being determined, students can gain a better understanding of the *F* word—failure. When presented with new tasks, they may encounter setbacks. Not all students see setbacks as an opportunity to learn, though. Many students need to develop the drive to persevere to achieve their goals despite many obstacles. Isn't that life, really? We all encounter barriers and have setbacks, but it's how we respond that determines the kind of learner we are. Through **reflection**, learners think about what is and isn't working and seek out feedback to improve.

Galileo Camps

STEAM and making don't solely happen in schools. Other organizations outside of the formal learning environment also contribute to the development of the Habits of Mind and the characteristics of innovative young people. The classroom poster referenced earlier was adapted from Galileo Camps (**http://www.galileo-camps.com/about/mission**), an organization with a great mission "to create a world of fearless innovators." Their *innovator's mindset* boils everything down to those five key characteristics.

Makerspace Bulletin Board

GRAPPLING WITH MAKING AND DESIGN

Embracing an innovator's mindset pushes learners to experience things beyond the traditional classroom. "I want the kids to fail," said Michael Penn (personal communication, January 2014), who serves as the lead instructor in the Shaler Area Elementary IKS Titan. He encourages students to jump into new challenges and give them a try. He knows that not every student will walk away successful, but it is often the reflection afterward that produces new learning benefits. These characteristics connect well with these phases of making.

Phase 1: Jump In

What Students Say: "I don't know what to make."

What Students Can Do: Brainstorm, make lists, plan, sketch

Mindset: Active engagement

Phase 2: Try Something

What Students Say: "I'm stuck."

What Students Can Do: Research, think, communicate with peers

Mindset: Flexible thinking, staying open to possibilities

Phase 3: Iterate

What Students Say: "This isn't turning out right."

What Students Can Do: Evaluate materials, get feedback, adjust design, revise plan

Mindset: Perseverance

Phase 4: Reflect and Seek Feedback

What Students Say: "I'm done. I like what I made. I'm not worried about what others think."

What Students Can Do: Listen, question, communicate, reflect, consider other options

Mindset: Receptive to input

Throughout the book, lesson ideas will be shared so classroom teachers can get started in STEAM Making. These activities will include basic information that could then be expanded to more complex units or challenges. Most will require everyday materials, not items that will require much of a budget. It is the goal that these "STEAM Maker Starters" will introduce some basic principles of making and design to students and teachers.

STEAM Maker Starter

Lesson: Get Moving!

Goal: Use the materials provided to design a vehicle that can move across the room using air power.

Timeframe: Minimum of 30 minutes

Possible Materials:

plastic water bottles (empty)	Play-Doh
toilet paper rolls	duct tape
straws	string
bottle caps	balloons
candy mints (with a hole in the middle)	rubber bands
old CDs	cardboard

Procedures: After you pose the challenge to students, allow individuals or groups to create a plan for their vehicle. Students can sketch on a notepad or design their model on a whiteboard. Allow for about 10 minutes to plan before having them select materials. Provide time for the building process. After about 15 minutes, you may want students (and you) to provide feedback to one another before returning to their models. Students are encouraged to try out their vehicles periodically and make adjustments. You may want to tape off an area on the floor for students to test their models.

Culminate the lesson once all models are complete. Students can gather together and watch as all vehicles are tested. The group can record which vehicles traveled the furthest, fastest, and so forth. To close the lesson, students can write a reflection on the design process and/or the success/failure of their model. A reflection sheet for this (or other tasks) can be found in Appendix G.

You may choose to show examples to your students before, during, or after the lesson. YouTube has several videos that show the building and testing of these vehicles (**https://www.youtube.com/watch?v=3Dw6N0Tn_sU**).

YouTube Balloon Car

ASSESSMENT

One of the barriers for educators with regard to implementing STEAM Making into their classrooms is the challenge of assessment. Programmed to use a paper-and-pencil test to determine proficiency, classroom teachers often struggle with how STEAM Making fits into their grade books. While there are strategies that can be considered when it comes to assessing this type of learning, the bottom line is if you are married to your teacher's manual and have the next five chapter tests already photocopied, then STEAM Making probably isn't for you. If you are open to the idea but need to find some ways to meaningfully assess this learning, then read on.

Student STEAM Maker

Leo was a kid who was failing and not in the positive sense of the word. He was struggling to pass his learning support classes, wasn't turning in homework, and was missing a lot of school. He seemed to lack motivation and was in jeopardy of being held back in fourth grade. He was not a student who demonstrated any particular affinity for sports or music; no one really knew what his hobbies were. As a struggling reader, he had a hard time in most of his classes, until the day he stumbled into the STEAM lab.

Leo's friend asked him to go with him to see some of the things he had been working on. After observing the space and checking out some materials, Leo asked if he was allowed to use some things in the woodworking corner. The teacher, who was facilitating in the lab, explained the criteria for using the woodworking tools. Leo put on his safety goggles and quickly started tinkering with a piece of wood, hammering away. He demonstrated more than just a basic knowledge of the tools. When the teacher recognized his abilities, he showed him the drills and array of saws. Leo was in his element!

Over the course of the next two weeks, Leo visited the lab every day at lunch. He ate his food quickly, then returned to his project. Leo's first project was a stool with an upholstered seat. He went on to design and build additional projects, which boosted his self-worth. The academic team soon saw increases in Leo's grades across several subject areas. Leo found something that he enjoyed and was really good at. STEAM Making was a breakthrough for him, as it has been for many students.

ALL INCLUSIVE

STEAM learning and making are for everyone. The inclusion of this practice makes learning accessible for any student with a disability. The hands-on nature makes it perfect for young learners in pre–K through Grade 2, who benefit from tactile tools and manipulatives. I've observed kindergarten classes weaving and constructing pulleys and levers. During our Family Reading Night, families with two- and three-year-olds flocked to our studio, where they heard stories and then built characters and settings inspired by the text.

This approach is meaningful for students with special needs as well. Students with a variety of abilities and disabilities thrive in a makerspace atmosphere or STEAM learning space. Students like Leo (a featured Student STEAM-Maker), who have learning disabilities in reading, may struggle in traditional classrooms that are text based. But in a hands-on environment, they can show what they know, well beyond what paper-and-pencil learning can demonstrate.

STEAM Making can also engage students with physical disabilities. Makerspaces offer a variety of experiences to meet the needs of the students. Perkins Learning shares STEM activities for students who are blind or visually impaired, deaf or hearing impaired at **http:// www.perkinselearning.org/accessible-science.**

Perkins Learning

Speech and Language

Other students, like those with speech and language challenges, can improve skills as they work on a project. Our speech therapist recently sent me a YouTube video of one of her sessions in our studio where she was working with three kindergarten students. As opposed to correcting articulation errors and developing expressive language in her office, she took the group to the studio to build with Rokenbok blocks. She was able to work on student goals like asking and answering "wh" questions:

- What can you build using only red blocks?

- Where can this rectangular block fit?

- Who might live in this block house that you've built?

For students with speech and language needs or those whose first language isn't English, STEAM Making offers a way for kids to connect with one another and share an experience even if it isn't through a verbal exchange. These experiences may be a springboard to develop student voice and give them a story to tell.

English Language Learners (ELL)

A makerspace can also be a breakthrough for students whose first language is not English. Building a roller coaster or designing a board game with ELL students is a great way to share an experience and generate opportunities for conversations. Hands-on experiences as well as learning in cooperative groups benefit ELL students. STEAM Making can give ELL students an opportunity to engage in learning that is fun while developing language.

For some students, schools are failing them. Restrictive curriculum, standardized programs, and inflexible schedules often don't meet the needs of students with learning disabilities, autism, speech and language needs, or those who are English Language Learners. STEAM and making offer meaningful possibilities for ALL students to engage in building, designing, and creating, while addressing individual goals for learning.

Students With Autism

Students with autism often benefit from experiences in STEAM Making. Students who have difficulty with social interaction, those who may be nonverbal, and others who need sensory input often enjoy visits to the STEAM Studio. Some students really find their niche there. Since autism can present in so many different ways, the hands-on approach to learning can really support those needs. As a student on the spectrum, Max found great success in a STEAM Making program in his school.

Max was disorganized. He didn't often understand social cues. He had a few friends but was not always included in games at recess. In the STEAM Studio, his was a different story altogether. Max was a leader. He knew every tool in the space. He could explain the intricacies of any coding program and was the resident robotics expert. All of the students consulted him for guidance. In this space, his confidence soared! With his self-esteem building, Max continued to develop peer relationships, which began to carry over into his classes and out into the community. His success continued as Max started mentoring younger STEAM Makers too! I often wonder how things might have turned out for Max had he not had this opportunity . . . had the school not had this space that allowed him to shine.

Technology is often a draw for students with autism. One tool that many students connect with is Minecraft. This online game may seem like just another video game, but it does provide opportunities for all students to use their imaginations and develop problem-solving skills as they create a 3-D world. Students can develop a sense of control and routine while they explore virtual worlds, which can benefit many types of learners. Learning and writing code are often favorites for students with autism.

STEAM and making are untapped opportunities for many learners. As more and more students and school dig into these topics, questions are beginning to emerge. One prominent question is surrounding assessment. How do teachers assess this learning? Should this learning be formally assessed? Will we see "making" on our report cards? How do we measure student understanding and mastery of STEAM and making? In public education, we know accountability is inevitable, so it is relevant to explore possibilities for assessing this new knowledge.

CREATING A BADGING SYSTEM

Badging in the classroom has the potential to be an effective learning tool (Ash, 2012; Pearson, 2014). A badging system, digital or physical, focuses learning with specific goals. Physical badges are not a new idea; the scouts have been embracing this idea for decades. If you want to earn your cooking badge, then you need to cook something. If you're interested in a sewing badge, then sew something. Learning by doing—a powerful method for both students and adults.

Badging can foster a collaborative learning environment, deepen student learning, and provide students with specific and immediate feedback (Cengage Learning, 2014). Looking for ways to increase student recognition? Badging is validating! It allows the learner to explore a topic in depth and then demonstrate their understanding of that learning. As students work toward a badge, they adjust, revise, and resubmit their work in order to meet the level expected. This approach fosters a deeper understanding of the task since it requires a demonstration to determine proficiency. It is also a practical way for students to share what they have learned with others. After earning a badge, students can then serve as an expert for that task.

·········· **Student STEAM Maker** ··

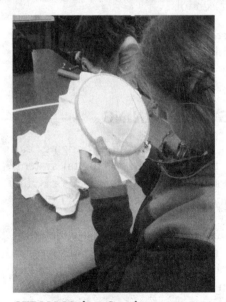

STEAM Maker Sewing

Madison had a lot of experience sewing at home. She understood how to use materials safely and demonstrated her knowledge to her teacher. At school, she quickly earned her badge for hand sewing as well as using the sewing machine. She sewed a small pillow by hand to demonstrate that she threaded a needle, performed various stitches, and finished off the piece. On the sewing machine, she created an apron. She threaded the bobbin and changed the color of thread for her project. Once she finished the items, she then modeled different techniques for her classmates and helped other students troubleshoot when working in the sewing area of her school's makerspace.

PHYSICAL BADGES

The STEAM Studio at Crafton Elementary started using a physical badge system as a way to monitor student use of new tools. A concern was expressed about using tools that could potentially be dangerous. How might the students demonstrate their capability to work in the studio without direct teacher oversight? Through some brainstorming, it was decided that students would need to meet certain criteria to show their proficiency in using various tools around the space. The criteria ensured that students had to uphold safety standards while also demonstrating skill. The studio posted a list of badges earned by students so that all staff would know who was able to use the tools. Many students wore their badges proudly as a symbol of their achievement. Scarves, necklaces, and pins adorned many student STEAM Makers. The appendix includes a list of badges and criteria for each badge used in the K–6 building. (You can find examples of physical badging in Appendix A.)

Harvard Business Review

DIGITAL BADGES

Digital badges are also trending. This online means of gaining new knowledge is accessible to learners in any area imaginable. Badging is a way to document and track learning through formal and informal pathways. In 2013, the *Harvard Business Review* named badging one of four innovation trends to watch for (**https://hbr.org/2012/12/four-innovation-trends-to-watc.html**). Institutions of higher education, businesses, and community organizations are recognizing the potential for badging beyond what is occurring in K–12 schools.

Mozilla Foundation

The Mozilla Foundation developed Open Badges (**http://openbadges .org**) as a way to collect, issue, and display digital badges.

Digital Badging

Source: Photo by Ben Filio, courtesy of The Sprout Fund.

CITIES OF LEARNING

Pursuing learning through badging can happen anywhere with the digital systems that are in place. In Chicago, Mayor Rahm Emmanuel initiated the Summer of Learning as a way to continue student learning after the school year ended. This citywide effort to offer meaningful learning pathways for young people resulted in 150,000 badges issued in the summer of 2013. Over 1,000 types of learning were explored across the city in formal and informal settings. More cities are joining this initiative as Pittsburgh, Washington, DC, Columbus, Dallas, and Los Angeles jump in for 2015.

SUMMARY

Badging in the classroom can lead to an improved quality of work, but it can also lead to the *F* word—Failure. The beauty of badging is students may have setbacks, they can continue learning until they earn their badge. It may take multiple attempts, but with perseverance, they will achieve!

As I pondered the title for this chapter, I wondered if readers would see "Fail" and have a negative impression. Though many teachers have shielded their students from it, failure is an important part of learning. Think about it—what does immediate success really teach our students? Sure, it's satisfying and builds confidence. What happens when that same student is faced with a complex challenge, one that requires multiple steps or extensive thinking and problem solving? Kids struggle with this! While it may sound punitive, we need to set our students up to fail. That is, we need to give them opportunities to grapple with things that don't come so easily for them. This is one reason why I believe that STEAM Making can be a powerful learning strategy. Today's students need exposure to solving problems that aren't "right out of the book." They need opportunities to question, argue, define, debate, research, and defend. Are these happening regularly in your classroom? If they are, then you are ahead of the game. If not, keep reading. You'll find examples from innovative schools in the next few chapters. These examples may be things that you can replicate in your school. Or they might give you a new idea for something that will be successful for your students in your school.

EXPANDING YOUR THINKING

In what ways do I give my students opportunities to fail that will encourage them to persist?

_____

_____

_____

_____

_____

How might I integrate the Habits of Mind into my instruction?

_____

_____

_____

_____

Reflect on one student in your class who struggles in the general curriculum. How would the inclusion of STEAM and making meet his or her individual needs?

_____

_____

_____

_____

_____

How might badging be used as an assessment in my school or classroom?

_____

_____

_____

_____

_____

CHAPTER 4

CoNNecT

An artist is a nourisher and a creator who knows that during the act of creation there is collaboration. We do not create alone.

—Madeline L'Engle

A noisy classroom at the end of the hall reveals a dozen third graders all over the floor. Some are arguing, others crawling across the space. The teacher is nowhere in sight. This is not a classroom management disaster. The students are on the floor testing out their model bridges that they've built over the last few weeks. Some are revamping their projects, while others are discussing ways to reinforce their base to make it stronger for their upcoming challenge. The teacher is on the floor too, consulting with a group. The children are thoroughly engaged in collaborating with their design team.

The Challenge

- Work in teams of three to four.

- Use a variety of reusable materials to build a bridge that can withstand the greatest amount of weight.

- Be ready to present your design plan, defend your choices, and share with the group any difficulties that you faced.

- Make one post on the class blog and respond to at least one other team's post about what you've learned from this task.

This example of an integrated lesson connects standards in math, science, engineering, speaking, listening, and writing using digital tools. Prior to the building phase, the teacher invited a local civil engineer in to talk with the students about designing bridges for strength. This created a connection of the content to real careers. The students learned about different types of bridges: beam, truss, arch, and suspension. The unit of study also built student vocabulary, as these eight-year-olds demonstrated an understanding of key content: arch, beam, deck, column, fixed arch, footing, portal, and strut. Living in a town of many rivers and bridges, the students were quickly able to connect this knowledge to their community, visiting local bridges and researching other famous bridges around the world. This is one example of the rigorous content and integrated units of study that students can engage at the elementary level.

It could be argued that this example is STEAM education only. The lesson provides hands-on learning that connects content in math, science, and engineering. The arts are included through the literature that students are exposed to and the aesthetics of designing a bridge that serves a purpose and has interesting visual elements. Technology is included through the student research of bridges as well as through their documentation on the class blog. So is this STEAM or making? If students were provided a bridge-building kit with premeasured planks, plastic connectors, and a picture or example of what the final product should look like, then it might be considered STEAM education. But in this case, the teacher allowed students to explore a variety of materials of all shapes and sizes to come up with a model of *their* choosing. Some had big dreams of soldering metal pieces into a bridge. Others envisioned taking a more traditional route with Popsicle sticks and glue. Some criteria existed to provide a goal for the students, but they were free to create using anything that they saw fit. The open-ended nature of this experience is one that I would categorize as STEAM Making.

In my experience, it is at the intersection of STEAM and making that the most creative outcomes exist. Over the course of several years, I have worked to embed the two into the instructional practices in my elementary school. Our team took meaningful steps toward connecting subject matter as well as the work we started in STEAM and linking it all to the idea of Maker Education. STEAM and making continue to transform learning, and schools are finding innovative ways to integrate these programs into their curriculum. Here's the path that our school took.

INNOVATIVE SCHOOL: CRAFTON ELEMENTARY

Bold blue paint covers the walls, along with photos and student work. Mobiles inspired by Alexander Calder hang from the ceiling. In one corner, a student-designed Rube Goldberg device sits as students prepare to make a revision to their model. Unique furniture is organized in small niches around the room. Neon green stools, futuristic yellow rocking chairs, and a bright blue couch serve as comfortable learning spaces for students. Bins and shelves are filled with buttons, fabric, wood scraps, motors, and LED lights. It is clear from the moment you enter the room that this is not an ordinary classroom but a distinctive space where learning is fun!

Along one wall is a bank of computers. Students often come in during "open studio" time—lunch and recess. They work on creating animated stories using Scratch or building their digital world in Minecraft. Ranging from beginner to very complex, a variety of robotics kits fill a large cabinet. Some students tinker with these. Some read the manual. Others jump right in and figure the program out for themselves. Many students have discovered they are able to create unique structures, programs, and processes that aren't included in the manual.

Crafton Elementary is a small, neighborhood school with approximately 350 students. From outside, the school shows its 100 years with elegant architectural details, but on the inside, the building boasts colorful classrooms and modern technologies. The school is a lively learning place filled with enthusiastic students and dedicated faculty and staff nestled in a small community that values education. In 2010, the school embarked on a new educational adventure.

It began with a request for proposals from a major funding group in Pittsburgh that intrigued the principal (me). The proposal was looking for schools that were interested in integrating science, technology, engineering, art, and math and wanted to pilot some program ideas. We submitted a grant, which started us on our way to becoming one of the early learning spaces dedicated to STEAM in our area.

The Crafton Elementary STEAM Studio provides opportunities for students to think critically, collaborate, and create authentic products in a technology-rich manner. Here, the learning opportunities promote creativity, open-ended exploration, problem solving, and real-world investigations. Over the last four years, this space has changed and transformed along with the instructional practices of the teachers. Once an empty classroom, the studio is a vibrant space for K–6 students and their teachers. The following sections describe the journey our school took over the course of several years to infuse STEAM and making into our practice.

YEAR 1

In the first year, the school was awarded $10,000 in competitive grant funding to integrate STEM into the school. That year, teachers worked with the Carnegie Science Center, bringing exploratory, hands-on learning into the classrooms. Science educators engaged students in experiments and problem-solving challenges, while teaching about physics, biology, and engineering. Earth and space science standards were addressed through collaborative activities on weather, the water cycle, air pressure, and landforms.

Coupling these learning opportunities with the need to increase literacy, nonfiction texts in math and science were added to the school's leveled library. This connection encouraged teachers to infuse more science into their general teaching, which was admittedly neglected in previous years because of standardized testing pressures. When an active learning task was paired with a high interest, informational text, students were more actively engaged in their reading. With the need for students to become close readers, this continues to be an important component of instruction.

A Polycom unit was also purchased so that classes could participate in videoconferencing. At the time, a local university was developing simulated, problem-based, learning adventures delivered via distance learning technology. These simulations, called e-Missions, integrated STEM subjects into an incredible, interactive learning experience. Now schools across the country link with the university to offer this type of learning to their students. Wheeling Jesuit University continues to develop e-Missions

e-Missions

for students in Grades 3 through 12. Its web site **http:// www.e-missions.net** provides information on the programs and shares a video of an e-Mission in action. The Polycom unit (back then, a pricey piece of equipment) connected students and teachers with other educators and experts across the globe. For us, videoconferencing was the gateway to integrating content areas in meaningful ways. It also served as a way to connect our students to the world.

Videoconferencing

Smithsonian National Air and Space Museum

Students can interact with the Smithsonian National Air and Space Museum without leaving the classroom! The museum offers interactive videoconferencing programs featuring the museum's staff and docent volunteers (**http://airandspace.si.edu/explore-and-learn/educator-resources**).

Wildlife Conservation Society

The Wildlife Conservation Society offers educational programs including videoconferencing opportunities with the Bronx Zoo (**http://www.wcs.org/teachers/distance-learning.aspx**).

NASA Digital Online Learning Network

The NASA Digital Online Learning Network connects students and teachers with NASA experts and education specialists using online communication technologies (**http://www.nasa.gov/audience/foreducators/#.VBBiHsJdWul**).

The Center of Science and Industry (COSI) connects your students with scientists, doctors, and experts in their fields (**http://www.cosi.org/educators/educator-ivc**).

Center of Science and Industry

Connect All Schools is a consortium of schools all over the world with a very specific goal: to connect every school in the United States with the world by 2016 (**http://www.connectallschools.org/home**).

Connect All Schools

Note: It may be helpful to cover other QR codes in this box with a sheet of paper to help focus your phone or tablet on a particular QR code.

Classes at all grade levels were able to use the technology to enhance their science, social studies, and math classes. Videoconferences were held for students with the San Diego and Indianapolis Zoos as well as with Candlestick Park, Yellowstone National Park, and the Grand Canyon. The equipment was used to join with classrooms in other states and other countries, communicating with children in places far away from Crafton. Talking with authors and illustrators became much easier with the videoconferencing equipment connecting classes with authors like Robert Munsch and Marc Brown. Serving as a tool for teachers as well, the technology was also used for professional development and training sessions throughout the year. Since then, hundreds of organizations have created videoconferencing programs for students. (See the sidebar above to explore other videoconferencing opportunities.)

STEAM Showcase of Learning

Our first year culminated with a special event to share our work with the school community. A Showcase of Learning was held to demonstrate the projects students did in the STEAM Studio. In its first year, the event was attended by hundreds of students, their families, and community members. In addition to the local school community, other school districts were also invited to the school to observe the project events. Students and teachers at each grade level presented projects. Classes did demonstrations, as well, presenting videos, while others participated in a live videoconference during the showcase.

This event created a buzz, which brought positive attention to the school. Soon, additional community and business partners became involved in the STEAM program. More parents asked to volunteer and got involved in school activities. Teachers also began to generate new ideas. Identifying local resources and engaging parents in the STEAM initiative helped to develop the program further.

Snap Circuit Rover

Source: Photo by Ben Filio, courtesy of The Sprout Fund.

For example, one fourth-grade parent worked for The Bayer Corporation, which supports STEM education through the Making Science Making Sense program. This free, hands-on program is facilitated by Bayer employees, who are required to volunteer their time to support local schools. (Google and other companies require employees to volunteer outside of the office. Find out which organizations in your area also encourage service in their employees.) The school utilized the Bayer program during the showcase as well as throughout the school year, with a learning station. See Bayer's website for more information (**http://www.msms.bayer.us/MSMS/ MSMS_Home.aspx**).

Because of another parent's affiliation with Pittsburgh Plate Glass Industries (PPG, **http:// corporate.ppg.com/Innovation/Science-Education.aspx**), the school secured additional funding for a hands-on science program about robotics. This has become an annual event where students attend an interactive assembly in the morning followed by hands-on learning stations in the afternoon. Stations are facilitated by parents and community members. Each year the topic focuses on one aspect of science: color and light, conservation, geology, robotics, and so forth.

Bayer

At the end of the first year, the tone throughout the school began to change. We were building momentum. Teachers began researching other ways to include more science and technology into their teaching. They took advantage of common planning time and attempted a more integrated instructional approach. Teachers also started looking at potential technology to bring into the classrooms. As a team, the faculty explored other grant opportunities looking for funding sources. Before the new school year began, the health and physical education teacher as well as the reading specialist were awarded their first educational grants to fund other innovative programs!

PPG

It's important to learn about STEAM so that we can have lots of opportunities in our future and to have a job in something we love.

—Taylor, age 12

In the 21st century, so many jobs will have STEAM in them.

—Natalie, age 11

I learned through the e-Missions and the Carnegie Science Center that with teamwork, you can get the job done!

—Brandon, age 10

I learned so much about science and space! The whole STEAM thing was really fun and I hope we can do it next year.

—Sam, age 10

YEAR 2

Crafton Elementary was headed in the right direction, but teachers lacked some of the resources to continue that momentum. While the Polycom unit was a great tool, there was only one. Some teachers didn't even have computers in their classrooms, let alone any extras. Seeing the importance in building technology into the curriculum, the district began to add Promethean Boards into the classrooms. District funds were also used to purchase laptops for intermediate students and ELMO cameras for several classrooms. As the teachers began to pilot these tools and find success, the demand increased. They were looking for ways to tap into student interest in technology, but district dollars only stretched so far.

K'NEX Model

Source: Photo by Ben Filio, courtesy of The Sprout Fund.

A small grant was used to purchase ActiVote systems for a few classrooms, pairing technology with formative assessment. These student response systems enabled teachers to poll students at any time during class to assess progress and, based on responses, tailor lessons to specific student needs. Students loved the novelty of this device, and it seemed to motivate them to participate, but the novelty was a part of the problem. This interest began to wear off. It was during this time that we realized that technology wasn't going to be enough. In order for creativity to be sustained, teachers needed to have a variety of tools and skills at their disposal. Professional development needed to be evaluated and the school needed to identify areas of interest for students and teachers. Student surveys revealed that students were interested in building and robotics. They were accessing numerous apps on iPads at home but had no access to these tools at school. Teachers had limited knowledge of iPads at the time and struggled to figure out how to include these interests in the existing curriculum. (Appendix B provides a sample professional development plan for schools starting a STEAM or making initiative.)

At this time, the Grable and Benedum Foundations were looking for schools to create dedicated spaces for learning. This was also around the time that STEM was shifting to STEAM. Twenty thousand dollar grants were awarded to five school districts around Pittsburgh. We submitted a proposal that included the idea of a dedicated space for STEAM learning. We used these funds to purchase materials and equipment for students and teachers to use in the STEAM Studio. Initially, we purchased a lot of commercial materials: K'NEX, Legos, and Snap Circuits were familiar to many

fischertechnik

students and made for an easy entry point for those who were unsure about the idea of design and engineering. A few advanced robotics kits were also purchased through fischertechnik (**http://www.fischertechnik.de/en/Home.aspx**). A class set of iPads combined with professional development from our local intermediate unit helped to get students and teachers engaged.

The initial goal was to create opportunities in the following areas:

- Mechanics and structures
- Scientific exploration and data collection
- Publishing and multimedia
- Robotics
- Circuitry
- Computer simulations

Students used K'NEX to build bridges, vehicles, and amusement park rides. Using these kid friendly materials, students really began to develop a foundation in engineering and design. "Just a toy" to outsiders, using manipulatives helped students to truly see the connection between what they were learning in class and the real world. They started to develop an understanding of the way bridges were built and how they could build a model with strength in mind. Students also explored systems and circuitry using Snap Circuits. Once a part of the fourth-grade science curriculum, now first graders were exploring basic circuits and demonstrating their knowledge by creating closed circuits. Squishy Circuits are a great start for primary classes to learn the basics about circuits as well (**http://www.makershed .com/products/squishy-circuits-kit**).

Squishy Circuits

Other students used their time in the studio to explore robotics, which was a brand new opportunity for most. Lego WeDo kits allowed students to use a familiar product and then create the code to program the model. For example, one group of students built a model of windshield wipers and then programmed them to start on a delay, wipe at a certain speed, pause, and then start again. Another group built a model of the Empire State Building and programmed the lights to blink on and off using a sensor.

All students had the opportunity to visit the STEAM studio with their class, but many students also gave up their lunch and recess to work together on projects. One group of sixth-grade boys built remote-controlled rovers and created obstacle courses to race through. Another group spent weeks deconstructing a microwave and other small appliances. They were completely intrigued with the interworking. (CAUTION: Make sure your students know what can and cannot be tinkered with! One classroom computer had a "broken" note on it for the computer technician. A student thought that meant it was fair game and he quickly took apart the hard drive.) Each month, I held a lunch session with the intermediate students and posed a design challenge, in addition to the time spent in the studio with their classes. Students could come into the studio and work on their projects up until challenge day. Challenges included building Rube Goldberg devices, marshmallow toothpick bridges, and marble runs.

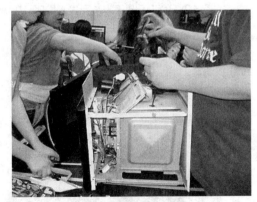

Deconstructing the Microwave

The students were very excited about the activities happening in the studio. One group started a petition to get programs at the junior high, where they would attend the following year! This wasn't the only example of students being propelled into action. Another group of students decided they would use their experience in STEAM Making to benefit others. Two fourth-grade students explored making wearable art, ornaments, and key chains during their time in the studio. They approached me to see if they would be able to sell the items in our school during lunch and recess. With a desire to give back and a passion for animals, the students decided that a portion of their sales would go to the National Wildlife Foundation, focusing on preventing the extinction of pandas. The early development of entrepreneurship is one idea that we continue to build on.

One unexpected outcome was that students started using materials in unintended ways. They took K'NEX pieces and added them to the robotics kits. They brought in PVC pipes to add to their marble run, which triggered a switch in the Snap Circuits set, ringing a bell to end their run. Toward the end of 2013, the school began to shift its work away from commercial materials (K'NEX, Legos, and Snap Circuits). While these served as a good entry point for student learning, the school began moving toward working with "real stuff." The MAKESHOP® in Pittsburgh and the Ignite Creative Learning Studio in California were the inspiration for a new focus in the STEAM Studio.

Over the summer, I responded to another request for proposals to serve as a mobile MAKESHOP® site. That August, a team of our teachers attended a "Maker Boot Camp," which provided professional development in woodworking, digital animation, sewing, and soldering. The experience was unlike any other training the teachers ever attended. The team returned to school in the fall invigorated and ready to implement new making experiences into the classrooms.

YEAR 3: MAKESHOP® YEAR

Because of some renovation work in the building, the STEAM Studio had to move locations. A different space with concrete floors ended up being the perfect place for the work that would transpire in Year 3. We were selected as a mobile site and elated to get the expertise from a resident maker once a week. Our MAKESHOP® Teaching Artist visited every Thursday, not only bringing expertise in making but also a love for learning. He was inquisitive, encouraging, and demanding. "No one shrugs around when you give them something to make. You can't beat those high levels of engagement" was a common mantra. With thanks to the museum, he brought lots of materials to get us moving. He didn't bring robotics kits or commercial materials but *real* stuff. From hot glue guns to batteries, motors, hammers, and saws, he held the belief that makers should be given

Robotics and Programming

Source: Photo by Ben Filio, courtesy of The Sprout Fund.

the opportunity to use the real thing. As a school, we began to see where making fit into our existing work with STEAM.

Our Teaching Artist offered professional development for teachers through "lunch and learn" sessions as well as after school. He used school time to team teach with classroom teachers and provide invaluable instructional coaching. He worked with teachers to brainstorm about projects and develop making experiences that connected to what the teachers were already doing in their classrooms. As a school, we began to look for curricular connections more deliberately, analyzing our reading programs and revisiting our test-prep materials. Sadly, an inevitable reality in public education, we aimed to make preparing for state assessments at least a little more meaningful. One standardized testing workbook included an article on Alexander Calder. This turned into a unit on designing and building mobiles in the studio. A story about turtles from the third-grade teacher's manual evolved into a turtle habitat project, including building model turtles from cardboard and other recyclables. Fourth-grade students designed kaleidoscopes based on the geometry they were learning in math. None of these were crafted with a kit or model. Ideas were developed and executed by students in an authentic way. In one short year, we went from using packaged products to going DIY using recyclable materials and household scraps. In Year 4 we would marry the two in a STEAM Maker approach that values the integrated nature of STEAM with the authentic experience of making.

What Are Teachers Saying?

Over lunch, several teachers and I had a conversation about STEAM Making in an effort to present a realistic look at the teacher's perspective in an instructional shift like this one. They thought back to when we started on our journey with STEAM Making. "We were essentially re-learning," clarified Health and Physical Education Teacher Josh Ficorilli. He pointed out the way he was instructed through his undergraduate training compared to the types of lessons teachers are implementing now. Fourth-grade teacher Andrea Mackey echoed a similar opinion, "We were always taught in college to give kids an example of what you wanted them to make. Here's a model of what it should look like. Our kids have been programmed to expect that, but we need to change that." Resnick and Rosenbaum (2013) caution STEAM Maker educators to avoid step-by-step recipes, as it takes away from student creativity and originality. The group chimed in, recalling similar experiences. With STEAM Making, we are pushing students to develop their creativity and think outside the box, but that can't happen if everyone is making birdhouses that mimic the model that the teacher has shown. While we used to value product more, the instructional shift is more toward the process now.

> It sounded CRAZY the first time my principal told us. But when you see the kids succeed, you know it works!
>
> — Adrienne Monaghan,
> fourth-grade teacher

Fifth-grade teacher Meghan Dettling finds the integration of STEAM and making to be the equalizer for students. "It helps students to see what others bring to the table." She goes on to share the ways she has watched students blossom as leaders and find their niche in the STEAM Studio. Students who were not traditionally leaders were stepping up. Other students were finding new things that they were interested in . . . and really good at!

What's the Hardest Part?

"You have to be OK with not giving set guidelines," explained Dettling. That was hard for a lot of teachers—turning some control over to the students. There's a risk when you leave things up to ten-year-olds. Mrs. Dettling and her colleagues began to shift the way they were providing instruction. They focused on three primary areas:

- Changing the way they asked questions
- Developing lessons that fostered collaboration
- Integrating subjects in a hands-on way

One project that resulted from these changes was a backyard design challenge. For the project, created by the fifth-grade team, the teachers transformed their existing units of math instruction into a series of performance tasks. The tasks focused on a fictional family that the teachers developed. Students would solve all sorts of problems revolving around the family—their weekly grocery shopping, the planning of their child's birthday party, and the remodeling of their home. Rather than presenting the traditional math unit on area, perimeter, and volume out of the manual, the teachers put the same content into a real-world scenario. Students developed their understanding of dimensions by determining how much carpet the family would need to purchase for their living room. Students used ads from home improvement stores to decide which paint brand would provide the best deal for the repainting of the family kitchen. Students calculated discounts and debated on whether the family should use a credit card or not, based on interest rates.

The year culminated with the ultimate backyard challenge, a group project that would incorporate math skills, along with the ability to collaborate with others. The task was to design a backyard space that met the criteria of the fictional family. The yard would need to be fenced in and include a deck as well as a play space for the children. Teams drew up the blueprints, ensuring accurate calculations. Once the blueprints were "approved," teams went to the STEAM Studio to start building. (Students were permitted to bring in items from home, but nothing could be premade. For example, teams couldn't use doll furniture; they had to build their items on their own.)

Students designed the outdoor space to include all of the requirements but also added their own unique touches. One group added lighting, while another created an in-ground pool. Others built a miniature swing set, outdoor furniture, and even a greenhouse. The teams had to work cooperatively, as the project had a designated timeline. As the deadline inched closer, teams began to prepare for the presentation of their design. Each group was required to present to an "expert panel," including a general contractor and interior designer, both volunteers from our community. The presentation also had to include a technology component. Several groups created a commercial for their design team, while others integrated the technology into the physical model. One group created a motorized merry-go-round that was the centerpiece for their backyard design. Students described their models, showing the panel the distinctive features of their design. The panel provided feedback to each group before choosing the winning design. The backyard design project has been done for the last three years and is now something that every fifth grader looks forward to.

STEAM Maker Teaching

"It takes time to get used to it. It is a new way of teaching," fourth-grade teacher Adrienne Monaghan expresses. The group of teachers also conveyed that it was a new way of learning for them. Fifth-grade teacher Anna Kostrick explains, "The first time WE had to be the makers in a professional development session, it was totally uncomfortable! It takes some getting used to . . . for everyone."

Teachers received ongoing training through district in-service trainings, lunch and learn sessions, and after-school professional development (PD). They explored PD beyond the school at neighboring districts as well as through the MAKESHOP's Maker Boot Camp. This week-long program is the ideal professional development opportunity for teachers who are new to making. It is a crash course in sewing, woodworking, electronics, and digital-based making. The Teaching Artists push participants out of their comfort zones to learn new skills, while also facilitating the development of a maker mindset.

> Things can be slow to change. If there is no autonomy, it is difficult for teachers to experiment.
>
> —Jesse Schell,
> CEO of Schell Games

While STEAM and making sounded fun, many struggled with implementing it in the classroom. "You have to wonder, how beneficial is this? With

Learning Stop-Motion Animation

all the outside pressures, is it really OK to devote time to this?" questioned teacher Tracy Alex. She was hesitant to integrate STEAM into her instruction but found "complete validation when you see what the kids can come up with!"

Health and Physical Education teacher Ficorilli interjects, "I thought you were crazy when you asked us to integrate this into our lessons! How can I do coding in gym class? How can I make this physical?" Collaborating with other teachers, Ficorilli designed an incredible unit for the Hour of Code (which ended up being more like 100 hours of coding, as opposed to just one). He used to his advantage the fact that students were learning basic coding in their general classrooms. They were using programs from the Code.org website that provided a foundation to the work they would add to in their weekly gym class. With a Minecraft theme, Ficorilli transformed the gym into a course that students would need to navigate by writing the code to maneuver their team through the simulated world brought to life.

Reading specialist Susan Kosko was cautious about straying away from her often-restrictive intervention lessons to venture into STEAM and making. When asked what she thought should be included in this book, she said, "I think you need to include a permission slip in the appendix. Teachers need to know that they have permission to try things that are different. Have your principal sign off that it's OK to think outside the box." (Thanks to Mrs. Kosko's suggestion, there is a permission slip in Appendix D. Give it to your principal or superintendent and get permission to move full STEAM ahead!)

Susan has spent the last few years connecting learning to the world. She believes, "it changes everything!" She has made "real-world" connections a priority in her classroom. Skyping with the Grand Canyon and participating in the Global Read Aloud, she has pursued opportunities that allow her students to think beyond the walls of our school. Read more about the global connections she has created in Chapter 6.

The teachers aren't blindly jumping on board. "A conflict exists—this is not how our kids are being tested," Jessica Bigler reminded the group. With the push for the Common Core State Standards and the reality of administering standardized tests for the entire month of April, the teachers understand that this is also a part of their responsibility. In Bigler's second-grade classroom, she has found a way to embrace innovation, while also preparing students to meet the standards. Inspired by a children's literature favorite, *Lilly's Purple Plastic Purse* by Kevin Henkes, her room boasts a "Light Bulb

Lab." This creative corner is a place where students can explore and design during center time. For about a half hour each week, the class visits the lab in small groups. Students designed blueprints for a zoo enclosure, made their own books, and built towers. This classroom corner devoted to students' abilities to pursue their interests connects to the project tackled by colleague Anna Kostrick.

STEAM Maker: Teacher Innovator

As the principal, I had been encouraging my teachers to become active on Twitter for a couple months when fifth-grade teacher Anna came into my office. "So, what do you think about this, Genius Hour?" Flexible and creative in her approach to classroom instruction, she began reading about Genius Hour on social media. This offshoot of Google's 20% time is a way for students to use an hour a week to pursue topics that they are passionate about. "Do you think it's OK? Can you help me?" Anna and I talked about what this would look like in her classroom, how she would communicate it to students and parents, and what she might need to get started.

> My principal was excited, so I was excited. I knew if it failed, it was going to be OK because it was a learning experience, so we started Genius Hour.
>
> —Anna Kostrick,
> fifth-grade teacher

Anna read some educational blogs and did some preliminary work before sharing the idea with her class. She determined that the students would need to have a clearly defined research question. In-depth logs with research notes were also required to ensure student accountability. In the fall, she launched her very own version of Genius Hour. Students chose topics with general approval from the teacher and were given an hour every Wednesday afternoon to research, question, discover, reflect, and pursue their passions. As the projects developed, changed, and grew, she pulled in mentors for student projects—a ballet teacher, someone from PNC Park, a researcher. One student researched her ancestry, going back several generations, finding documents from Ellis Island. Another student studied the history of dance and performed as a culmination of her exploration.

Each teacher took a different approach to STEAM Making, depending on each one's grade level or subject area. While each chose a different path, all at least took the risk. The outcome for all was an increase in student engagement. The final takeaway from our conversation: Start small. All of the teachers agreed, "try one thing." Add a maker activity to your favorite reading story or include a building challenge in your next math unit. Appendix C has a chart that might help you get started.

YEAR 4

With our building finishing its final phase of renovation work (a new office and secured entrance, new flooring and the completion of an HVAC project) the STEAM Studio moved again! (This goes to show you that makerspaces or learning labs, or whatever you call them, can be flexible and even mobile. If your space needs to move, it can!) We transferred the furniture, storage cabinets, and tools to a new room. The larger space with more storage was ideal. We also added a dry erase calendar outside the door. Classes could sign up to use the space as their individual schedules permitted. While no requirement was set, most classes visited the studio on a regular basis, some once a week and others every day for several weeks in a row.

This year would be different, though, with no Teaching Artist to guide us on our way. Would we make the shift and pursue these opportunities independently? I wasn't sure. There had to be some way to build internal capacity so that teachers were adding to their knowledge base.

Up until this point, STEAM and making were isolated to one building in our district. I was charged with the expansion of our program to include another elementary school. Building capacity for creativity and innovation had been a slow process in our building, developing over the previous three years. How in the world would this work translate to a school that had not engaged in this at all? After a brainstorming session with fellow principal, Carla Hudson, we proposed a "coaching position" that would allow a few interested teachers in her school to get involved and share our adventures in STEAM Making.

STEAM Facilitators

With help from a state grant, the district set aside funds to offer teachers a stipend to facilitate STEAM and making activities during lunch and recess. Ten teachers applied and agreed to share the responsibilities in each building. One stipulation was that teachers had to agree to attend one professional development session each month. The sessions, led by experts from the MAKESHOP®, focused on different topics including

- Scratch
- Stop-motion animation
- Design thinking
- E-textiles

While the sessions were mandatory for facilitators, they were available to all teachers. The informal, hands-on sessions were well attended by many teachers, thus spreading expertise in areas across teachers of many grade levels and content areas. (For example, our physical education teacher earned his badge in soldering. He was then able to serve as a model for others interested in learning to solder.)

By fostering teacher interest in other areas, internal capacity was building. A number of additional projects have emerged at Crafton Elementary since then. In the spring of 2014, the Girls with Gadgets project was created. After extensive work in the STEAM Studio, fourth-grade teacher Andrea Mackey wanted to provide additional learning opportunities for female students in her class. Many had already expressed an interest in learning more about building and design. She saw a Super Bowl ad for GoldieBlox and was so excited about the potential of this product to engage more young girls into engineering. She applied for a grant from the Female Alliance for STEM Excellence (FASE) to establish a program targeted at elementary school girls.

She created a lunchtime program in which students were able to learn about architecture, design, engineering, and robotics. She used the funds to purchase materials like GoldieBlox (**http://www.goldie blox.com**) and Roominate (**http://www.roominatetoy.com**), both marketed specifically to girls.

GoldieBlox

The kids were excited when they were able to watch the episode of Shark Tank that featured the products they were using in the STEAM Studio every day.

All twenty-four of the fourth-grade girls chose to participate in the program, which culminated with a visit to the Carnegie Science Center. The program continues to be offered to students in Grades 3 through 6, with an ongoing emphasis on opportunities for girls.

Roominate

Student STEAM Maker

Tara was a quiet fifth-grade student. She was strong academically and always passed every test with flying colors, but active participation was not her strong suit. She'd write beautiful essays and provide detailed answers to every word problem assigned, but she wouldn't share work with her class. An invitation to a lunchtime club changed everything for Tara. She started coming out of her shell after a few sessions with the Girls with Gadgets Club.

The all-girls setting put her at ease. She laughed and started to join in the conversation. She collaborated with other budding engineers, building a carousel, a dunk tank, and a model home. Tara spent two years in the club, culminating in her presentation at a school board meeting. The student who was once afraid to contribute to a class discussion was now enthusiastically promoting the Girls with Gadgets Club and showing off her projects to the larger school community.

Career Ready

Another program that developed through our STEAM Making efforts were "career talks." During the winter months when students are not able to be outside during recess, a series of career talks were set up for students in Grades 5 and 6. Professionals in various STEAM Making fields were invited in to talk with students about their educational background and chosen career path. The students were able to talk with nurses, patent attorneys, civil engineers, video game designers, and researchers. Many were parents, some community members, and others were relatives of the teaching staff. Students posed detailed questions to the speakers and developed a basic understanding of each field. Continuing this program not only brings parents and community members into the school but also helps students to learn about opportunities in STEAM fields for college, career, and beyond.

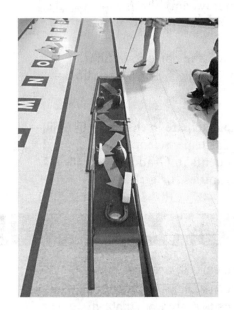

STEAM Maker Miniature Golf

Week of Making

With the call from President Obama, school districts and other organizations across the country participated in the week of making. June 12 through 18, 2015, was designated as the first week for making, coinciding with the National Maker Faire in Washington, DC. In response, I put the call out to our school. "The President is counting on you!" I implored them. What was the result? A nine-hole miniature golf course in the gym and a custom-made shelving unit for the STEAM Studio. Our health and physical education teacher takes challenges seriously, so when I put it out there that everyone should be making, he jumped on board. Various classes in Grades 3 through 6 designed and built their own holes for the course using recyclable materials as well as a variety of equipment from the gym. The designs that the students came up with were incredible! Throughout the week, students at all grade levels were able to play the golf course as a part of their gym class.

In addition to the masterpieces created by students for students, the fifth-grade class also built a shelving unit for the STEAM Studio. Always looking for places to put unfinished projects, the students decided to create a space themselves. With some help from teachers they used SketchUp to design the shelving unit, did all the necessary calculations, and got to work. Students measured twice and cut once, all of the pieces to the unit. They nailed each piece together, building the unit almost like a puzzle. The end result was spectacular.

Developing Resources

Another outcome from our journey becoming STEAM Makers was the development of meaningful resources. Through collaboration and ongoing dialogue about STEAM Making, we collected a variety of tools to help every teacher.

Week of Making

Every school has them—those teachers who will get on board enthusiastically no matter what initiatives come their way. (Probably you, if you are reading this book!) These teachers are the ones who arrive early and stay late, looking for whatever they can to motivate and engage their learners. These movers and shakers are the ones that are going to transform their classrooms and schools into centers for STEAM and making.

But in reality, time constraints, lack of resources, and testing pressures often pull even the best teachers away from providing opportunities to enhance creativity. What effective teachers look for is a way to make this type of learning fit into things that are already happening in the classroom. While STEAM Making can certainly happen in isolation simply for the purpose of creating something new, it is more meaningful for students when the making experience connects to other content. An easy entry point for many teachers, children's literature that lends itself to creative thinking, can be used regularly in the elementary classroom.

STEAM Maker Shelf

Table 4.1 lists books that can be used to support STEAM and making; books on robots, inventors, architecture, and so forth.

Now, let's think deeper than that! There are so many great stories that you are probably already reading in your classrooms right now that can inspire innovation in your students. Table 4.2 includes great children's books that tell engaging stories, while developing the imagination of your students. Not only can these books be used to develop vocabulary and comprehension,

TABLE 4.1 STEAM Maker Books by Topic

TOPIC	TITLE	AUTHOR
Architecture	*Architecture According to Pigeons*	Speck Lee Tailfeather
	Look at That Building	Scot Ritchie
Inventors and inventions	*Girls Think of Everything: Stories of Ingenious Inventions by Women*	Catherine Thimmesh
	Mistakes That Worked	Charlotte Jones
	Out of Darkness: The Story of Louis Braille	Russell Freedman
Robots	*My Robot*	Eve Bunting
	Recycled Robots: 10 Robot Projects	Robert Mallone
	My Robots: The Robotic Genius of Lady Regina Bonquers III	Johan Olander
Electricity	*Oscar and the Bird: A Book About Electricity*	Geoff Waring
	Electricity: Bulbs, Batteries, and Sparks	Darlene Stille and Sheree Boyd
	Energy Makes Things Happen	Kimberly Brubaker Bradley and Paul Meisel
Coding and programming	*Kodu for Kids: Official Guide to Creating Your Own Video Games*	James Floyd Kelly
	Adventures in Minecraft	David Whale
	Computers for Kids	Chris Cataldo
	Lauren Ipsum: A Story About Computer Science and Other Impossible Things	Carlos Bueno
Math	*Length*	Henry Arthur Pluckrose
	How Big Is a Foot?	Rolf Myller
	Mathterpieces	Greg Tang
	Patty Paper Geometry	Michael Serra

TABLE 4.2 Children's Literature to Support STEAM Makers

BOOK	AUTHOR	MAKE IT!	A LITTLE INSPIRATION	QR CODE
A Perfectly Messed-Up Story	Patrick McDonnell	Create your own unconventional book.	www.mutts.com	**Mutt's Comics**
Max Found Two Sticks	Brian Pinkney	Design and make musical instruments.	http://www.kinderart.com/teachers/9instruments.shtml https://making multicultural music.wordpress .com/2012/04/10/14 -world-music-instruments- that-can-be-made-from- recycled-materials	**KinderArt**
Mix It Up!	Hervé Tullet	Explore the mixing of colors through painting.	Try a paper towel chromatography project: http://pbskids.org/ zoom/activities/sci/ papertowelchromatogr .html	**PBS KIDS**
Koko's Kitten	Dr. Francine Patterson	Create a diagram or build a model of Koko's enclosure.	*The One and Only Ivan—* STEM Engineering Challenge via https://www.teachers payteachers.com/Store/ Smart-Chick	**Teachers Pay Teachers**
Stanley the Sock Monster Goes to the Moon	Jetta Robbard	Create an idea board for a potential project. Design and build a rocket.	Storyboard That is a free online tool that students could use to plan any design project: http://www.storyboard that.com	**Storyboard That**
Extra Yarn	Mac Barnett	Explore with yarn—weaving, sewing, knitting.	Hands-on activities connected to children's literature: http://playfullearning.net	**Playful Learning**
Number the Stars	Lois Lowry	Create a coat of arms as a symbolic representation of themselves.	The Medieval Classroom has various resources for classroom teachers: http://www.theme dievalclassroom.com.au	**The Medieval Classroom**

(Continued)

Note: It may be helpful to cover other QR codes in this table with a sheet of paper to help focus your phone or tablet on a particular QR code.

TABLE 4.2 (Continued)

BOOK	AUTHOR	MAKE IT!	A LITTLE INSPIRATION	QR CODE
Iggy Peck, Architect	Andrea Beaty	Design and build a _____ (castle, bridge, skyscrapers, tower, church, monument, etc.) from the story.	Check out author Andrea Beaty's Pinterest page for great ideas: https://www.pinterest.com/ andreabeatypint	**Andrea Beaty's Pinterest Page**
Where Do Frogs Come From?	Alex Vern	Design and build frogs that can jump.	Try the Origami Fun App or http://www.instructables .com/id/Origami-Jumping- Frog-VIDEO	**Origami Jumping Frog Video**
Junkyard	Mike Austin	Use recyclable or found materials to create a robot or other sculpture.	Some inspiration pics from amazing artists can be found at http://www.hongkiat .com/blog/recycled-art- masterpiece-made-from- junks	**Hongkiat**
Lilly's Purple Plastic Purse	Kevin Henkes	Design and sew a purse. OR Establish a *light bulb lab* in your room.	Easy projects for makers who want to sew are available at http://crazylittleprojects .com/2014/08/ quickandeasysewingprojects .html	**Crazy Little Projects**
The Most Magnificent Thing	Ashley Spires	Through perseverance and iteration, develop a vehicle to serve a special purpose.	http://www.scholastic .com/teachers/top- teaching/2014/10/design- thinking-lesson-connects- classmates	**Scholastic**
Gingerbread Baby	Jan Brett	Create puppets and put on a puppet show.	Jan Brett has a great website: http://www.janbrett.com	**Welcome to the World of Jan Brett**
Stuck	Oliver Jeffers	Design a contraption to help Floyd get his kite out of the tree.	http://www.teaching ideas.co.uk/library/books/ stuck.htm	**Teaching Ideas**
Henry's Amazing Machine	Dale Ann Dodds	Build a machine out of recyclable materials.	Read *More Picture-Perfect Science Lessons: Using Children's Books to Guide Inquiry*	

BOOK	AUTHOR	MAKE IT!	A LITTLE INSPIRATION	QR CODE
The Miraculous Journey of Edward Tulane	Kate DiCamillo	Re-create a scene from the story for Reader's Theater including creating costumes, scenery, props, backdrop.	There are lots of resources surrounding this *Global Read Aloud Book* from 2014: http://www.edwardtulane.com https://www.pinterest.com/emilyhstarkey/miraculous-journey-of-edward-tulane	**Edward Tulane** **Edward Tulane Pinterest**
Shh! We Have a Plan	Haughton	Learn about the design process.	PBS Design Squad http://pbskids.org/designsquad	**PBS Design Squad**
The Great Kapok Tree	Lynne Cherry	Build a model of the layers of the rainforest.	Here's a great Prezi with a link to a fascinating YouTube video: https://prezi.com/phhl2comcrpf/the-great-kapok-tree/#	**The Great Kapok Tree Prezi**
Not a Box	Antoinette Portis	Use recycled materials to create a "not a" story; for example, not a button, not a battery, not a thread.	Try these bookmaking websites to design and publish books: http://www.storyjumper.com https://www.mystorybook.com https://storybird.com	**Storyjumper** **My Storybook** **Storybird**
The Boy Who Harnessed the Wind	William Kamkwamba	Build a windmill.	http://tryengineering.org/lesson-plans/working-wind-energy http://learn.kidwind.org/learn/science_fair_projects	**Try Engineering** **KidWind**
Coppernickel, The Invention	Wouter Van Reek	Use the design process to create an invention.	http://www.playingbythebook.net	**Playing by the Book**

This activity could be used as a starter lesson for students *or* as a professional development activity for teachers. (My two cents: I used this idea as a back-to-school session with my teachers, as a way to integrate problem solving, collaboration, and a bit of design thinking.)

Lesson: Game Hack

Goal: As a team, create an original game with rules and procedures.

Timeframe: A minimum of 45 minutes, but could be extended over multiple class periods for students.

Materials: A variety of game items including game boards, game pieces, dice, spinners, cards, and so forth (hit the local thrift shop or area garage sales and buy a bunch of used or broken games: Life, Monopoly, Parcheesi, and other board games work well); also provide markers, scissors, glue, tape, sticky notes, and so forth

Procedures: Teams of three to four will work together to hack a game. They can choose existing game board and pieces to create a new game. They should create a theme, record their rules, and determine the procedures that players will follow.

Games could be created around a specific subject area or topic: "Today, everyone will make a math game." Or games could be created for younger students: "We will create a game for our kindergarten buddies, so that they can practice their letters and sounds."

Once all teams have completed their games, each should present to the large group. Time should be allotted for teams to play the new games created by the other groups.

Throw in a curve ball once groups have begun to construct their game and allow one team member take any piece/item from another team to add to their own game.

Reflection: Provide feedback to other teams: What did you like best about their game? What was confusing/unclear?

but they can also extend student thinking in the world of building, designing, and making. Want to get started but not sure where to begin? Just choose a book. If you need an idea, some are listed, as are websites that provide additional inspiration. Once you read a few of the books, you'll probably begin to generate great ideas on your own.

Obstacles

Having a dedicated space is both a blessing and a curse. With a large room and lots of storage, we thought our problems were solved, but student projects and donated materials soon overwhelmed the room. With no one person in the room permanently, things like organization, ongoing projects, inventorying materials, and cleaning were shared between everyone. We bought more and more bins and started labeling everything. We also keep an ongoing message board in the front of the room so everyone can communicate with one another. If someone uses the last of something, he or she writes it on the board: "Need more copper wire." If a project is unfinished and might look like a pile of scraps to someone else, a note goes on the board: "Please save my _____." Also, with help from our fifth graders, we have a new shelf to house and display projects.

Growing Ideas

Our next big step is going to be to add an entrepreneurial component to the program. Last year, on the way home from a field trip to the Carnegie Science Center with a group of fifth- and sixth-grade students, they asked if we could get a 3-D printer. I explained to the group how much money that would cost and how much I had in my budget. "We'll raise the money!" they shouted. The students exploded with ideas for what they could make and sell. "We could make candles and sell them for the holidays. We could build toys for younger students or even fix toys that are broken. We could make cards that light up . . . and shirts and bracelets!" They were on a roll. We plan to tap into that interest in the fall with plans for a holiday art show and exhibition, where students will sell items to add new things to our STEAM Studio.

SUMMARY

Every school that engages in STEAM and/or making will take its own approach. All teachers will find their own entry point. All students will find their niche. No path is exactly the same, which makes writing a book about the topic a challenge. Our journey at Crafton Elementary was a unique one, but it serves as only one example for integrating STEAM Making. Over time, we were able to connect the two ideas together; to what is now a STEAM Maker approach, one that values the natural connections between science, technology, engineering, art, and math, but also the open-ended, authentic philosophy of making. The connection between the two has powerful potential when it comes to advancing student learning (Bevan, Petrich, and Wilkinson, 2015).

EXPANDING YOUR THINKING

What connections can I create between STEAM and making in the classroom?

_____

_____

_____

_____

_____

_____

_____

How might I incorporate Genius Hour or a Light Bulb Lab into my classroom or school to inspire innovation?

_____

_____

_____

_____

_____

_____

_____

What obstacles may be in my way? What are some potential solutions?

_____

_____

_____

_____

_____

_____

_____

CHAPTER 5

Bu*i*ld

The secret of change is to focus all of your energy not on fighting the old, but on building the new.

—Socrates

A handful of second graders crowd around a table as they prepare to demonstrate a "draw-bot" that they built using littleBits (**http://little bits.cc**). The seven-year-olds described what they used to build it. They talk about the challenges they encountered along the way. "We didn't have things connected the first time and nothing happened!" One student explained to a group of adults touring the school, "We actually had to try a couple of designs before we got it working." These young makers understood the design process and the iterations often needed to build something impressive.

littleBits

Building something great takes time and effort. School districts across the country are building in many ways. Students are engaging in the physical building of outdoor learning spaces, battery-powered cars, and model cities for the future. Teams of teachers are building relevant curriculum to include courses in gaming and *Genius Hour*. District leaders are building a new culture, one that embraces creativity and innovation both in and out of school. Cities are building networks for learning that are supporting children and young adults as they pursue their passions.

Drawbots

THE ELLIS SCHOOL

Ellis is a private school for girls, right outside the city of Pittsburgh, serving 400 students in pre–K through twelfth grade. While the school has always maintained an excellent reputation for strong academics, it is now being recognized for its work in STEAM education. "We don't call it STEAM, we call it STEM-X. We focus on computational thinking, writing, and communicating," their dynamic leader, director of learning and innovation Lisa Abel-Palmieri told me on a visit in February of 2015. We toured the campus as she introduced me to colleagues, shared student work, and told me about the innovative things happening at Ellis.

"We've really moved from passive to active learning." This is evident as teachers have moved to an eighty/twenty lab-to-lecture model. Teachers are tinkering with flipped classrooms and Google Glass, developing lab casts for homework. With technology

Ellis Gallery

in the hands of teachers and students, the school has observed a more collaborative work ethic. The school itself is very student centered, with displays of student work in locations all over the campus. One hallway serves as an art gallery that the Upper School students curate each semester. Over the course of the last few years under Abel-Palmieri's tenure, the school has shifted toward advancing opportunities for young women in design thinking. This has occurred through opportunities in STEAM and making.

Big Ideas in Innovation

- Active, personalized learning
- Teacher as facilitator
- Human-centered design
- Community-connected learning
- Authentic, performance-based assessments

"Engaging girls in STEM—it's all about attitude," Abel-Palmieri told me during that same 2015 visit, and with that in mind, created the Tinker Squads after-school program for students in Grades 5 through 8. At that transitional age, she knew it was important to keep girls engaged in and out of school. "We've increased the content and saw an increase in engagement. We've found more risk-taking, confidence, and connections to the outside." The Tinker Squads program was an opportunity for students to work collaboratively while developing a growth mindset and building competencies in design thinking and making. The teams of girls used design thinking to solve problems in their community. After a successful pilot year, they expanded the program to reach out to other schools and organizations, representing various neighborhoods around the city. Ellis teachers served as mentors for these partners.

One organization, Assemble, is a unique community space for art and technology. Ellis partnered with Assemble to create a Tinker Squad at their facility, too. (Read more about Assemble in Chapter 6.) Two other schools jumped on board as well. Adding another layer of mentorship, high school students from the Girls of Steel program (**http://www.frc.ri.cmu.edu/girls ofsteel**) served as mentors. (This all-female robotics team works through Carnegie Mellon University, allowing students to learn about engineering and robotics and participate in competitions.)

Girls of Steel

Abel-Palmieri and other school leaders posed a challenge to their Tinker Squad students: Identity a problem in the community and solve it through making. All squads would gather at a Tinker meet to share ideas and earn digital badges. To prepare students for the challenge, experts in the field were brought in to support the students—a roboticist, an industrial design architect, and a local fine artist. Students planned projects that could take away trash, reduce stress, and assist community cyclists.

Invent-abling Kits

Students determined what materials they would need to solve their problem. They were provided "Invent-abling kits" (**http://teknikio.com**) to get started. The kits included switches, electronics, fabric, motors, lights, and batteries. On a Saturday morning, the squads met up at the Pittsburgh Center for Creative Reuse (see box) to gather additional materials. Students chose their materials, then went back to their schools to begin the building process before reconvening at a culminating event where students shared their designs. The Tinker Squad program was so successful that it is also being offered as a summer program at Ellis as well as being replicated in several other schools.

Tinker Squads

More information about Tinker Squads can be found at Sprout's website: **http://hivepgh.sproutfund.org/project/tinker-squads**.

Pittsburgh Center for Creative Reuse (http://pccr.org)

Pittsburgh Center for Creative Reuse

In this shop, artists, teachers, and community members can get all sorts of materials for projects. From computer parts to metal scraps, glass tiles, and random odds and ends, this place is a maker's dream! They even have a mobile component affectionately named "Fancy, the Robot Reuse Mobile," a van used to rescue awesome materials before they are sent to landfills as well as to travel to programs throughout the community.

In addition to Tinker Squads, Abel-Palmieri facilitates learning for students and adults in other ways. "We've become more intentional with regard to the interdisciplinary aspect," she explained. Teachers are working to develop connections between subject areas. These connections occur within the classrooms but also in other ways. She also facilitates STEAM Making with students. "We held a student competition to redesign spaces around the school. From thirty-eight places, they voted on one design." Students explored the campus, looking for areas to improve. Teams submitted their design proposals and everyone voted. Students ordered the furniture and even put everything together. Named the "Collaboratory," the room is a great space for groups to meet, both students and adults.

**Innovation Station
Intermediate Grades**

Innovation Station Primary Grades

Ellis's leadership has also built in time to enhance student-learning opportunities in more informal ways. Students in Grades 5 through 12 have time in between classes to collaborate—envision study halls that take place throughout the building in wonderful little learning nooks. There's a bar in one hallway with a few laptops where students can research, and comfortable furniture arranged in corners for study groups. The school also interspersed *innovation stations* around the building. At the end of hallways and even within some classrooms, the stations provide opportunities for hands-on learning using Legos, Cubelets, and other building materials.

During the school visit, one teacher talked about some of the cross-disciplinary work happening with her team. First-grade students created fishing poles and are reading about magnetism. Second-grade classes are learning about simple machines using Legos and presenting them in class. She shared a story about a recent adjustment that had to be made to one of their recent units of study.

A common task among schools is to design a compartment or contraption to safely drop an egg without breaking it. One child was allergic to eggs, which meant students couldn't complete the traditional egg drop experiment. Instead, students designed a mechanism to mail a potato chip. One teacher even wrote a short story about the chip and why it needed to be mailed across the country. Students read the book together and designed their contraptions. It was so well received that the potato chip project will replace the egg drop permanently.

Turtle Art

Another teacher describes some of the things his team is doing to integrate technology into their work in language arts and math. Ellis fourth graders are using Turtle Art (**http://turtleart.org**) to learn coding, giving directions in geometric terms. Inspired by LOGO programming, Turtle Art allows students to create a sequence of commands by connecting blocks of code together. The turtle follows the sequence, which in turn creates a graphic representation.

Hummingbird Kit

Students in Grade 4 also read the novel *Poppy* by Avi. Rather than drafting a written summary or a book report, students created dioramas of a scene using Hummingbird robotics. (The Hummingbird Robotics Kit is a tool that came out of a research project at Carnegie Mellon's CREATE Lab (**http://www.hummingbirdkit.com**). Students added LED lights and moving parts to represent Mr. Ocax and his interactions with Poppy.

The school also promotes several "interdisciplinary days," where teams create connected units that unite all subject areas. The fifth-grade students used their knowledge in history class on Ancient Egypt and combined that with the physical properties of matter from science class and their background in engineering to design Egyptian playgrounds. The project, grounded in human-centered design, pushed students to consider the people who would use their design.

Human-centered design includes developing empathy with the people you're designing for through four steps:

- Generating ideas
- Building a prototype
- Sharing the design
- Getting your idea out to the world.

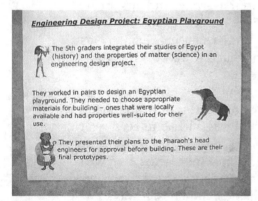

Egyptian Playground Design Project

Obstacles

One of the obstacles at Ellis was getting the instructional practices in STEM-X to grow. Recognizing the importance of advancing their program, teachers in the school have been named as "Innovation Fellows." These lead teachers are provided release time in an effort to move initiatives forward. The current focus is on educational technology, cross-disciplinary learning, and STEAM. The fellows meet regularly with one another and with school leadership to develop programs and integrated learning opportunities to meet the needs and interests of their students. They can also use their release time to plan instructional units, collaborate with colleagues, or co-teach a lesson.

Growing Ideas

The next step for The Ellis School includes hosting a conference this summer. The Active Learning and Design Thinking Summit is one of the projects from the school's Learning Innovation Institute. The goal of the Summit is to bring educators together to explore personalized learning and the growth mindset. Inspiration talks by Thomas Steele Maley and Grant Lichtman are planned for the event. In addition, regional leaders will facilitate "Leaders Lead" sessions to discuss alternative assessments, gaming, STEAM, and making.

········· STEAM Maker Starter ·········

Lesson: Build Something Magnificent

Goal: Engage in the design process to create something that is useful to students

Timeframe: Several lessons over an extended period of time

Possible Materials:

cardboard, plastic bottles, cap, cans, or other clean recyclables

scraps of paper or fabric

beads, buttons, or other small craft items

Procedures: Read aloud *How to Make a Magnificent Thing* by Ashley Spires. The story tells of a young girl and her dog trying to make something magnificent. The character struggles as she works through several steps of the design process. The story allows students to see that frustration is OK and the end result can be something wonderful. The character eventually creates a sidecar for her dog—something very useful for her.

Students will brainstorm possible inventions that would be useful to them. Keeping a notebook to sketch ideas or create lists might be helpful for students. Ideas can be shared with the teacher, a partner, or design team. After sharing, students can revise their designs or change their plan. Student building and design may occur over multiple classes, as needed. Students will return to the notebooks to reflect on the process, ask questions, and note changes.

As a culmination, all of the "magnificent things" should be presented and shared in some way.

As you are finding through the stories in this book, STEAM Making is not a one-size-fits-all practice. Every school will need to find a procedure and schedule that works for them. Here are a few school-wide options:

1. **Open Schedule.** Teachers may sign up on their own to use the STEAM Maker space or borrow the materials cart (or whatever your school is using).

2. **Rotation Schedule.** Some schools facilitate STEAM Making on a rotation, just as students would go to music, art, or physical education class.

3. **Library Makerspace.** With many schools using the library as a way to engage students in this work, this is a great drop-in space where students and teachers can visit anytime.

At the classroom level, many teachers are finding ways to incorporate STEAM Making into their daily practice. This can occur in an integrated manner, connecting STEAM Making experiences to children's literature or existing curriculum components. It may also be done as a stand-alone class or activity. Some teachers devote a period each week to work on hands-on projects.

Bottom Line. Create the schedule that works for you and your students. Experiment with times, locations, and classes until you find the best model for you!

ELIZABETH FORWARD SCHOOL DISTRICT

With visits from Thailand, Singapore, and districts around the northeast United States, the Elizabeth Forward School District is moving rapidly in the right direction. Once a rural district with traditional courses, Elizabeth Forward (EF) is now a leader in innovative programs. Early on, the district's strong leadership team provided a vision for innovation and technology in their schools. During a recent district tour for over 100 educators, super-intendent Bart Rocco stated, "Our district has two big theories—connect with people and give back." As stewards for innovative learning in the Pittsburgh region, they are fulfilling those goals.

Tours at EF are conducted monthly (since the demand has been so high) and include visits to three district buildings, one at each level. The high school boasts a newly renovated library and media center, gaming room, and fabrication lab. The middle school serves Grades 5 through 8 and is a model for many area elementary, middle, and high school programs.

STEAM Making in the Middle Grades

Just the sound of it makes it a place that any young person would want to learn—The Dream Factory. This dedicated wing in the EF middle school has been a space to foster 21st century learning, with classes in technology education, visual arts, and computer science. Computer programming is offered to all sixth graders, with seventh graders taking robotics. In *tech ed*, students create projects using the laser cutter, CNC router, and 3-D printers. They study the fundamentals of manufacturing, working with materials like wood, sheet metal, and plastic. Art classes go beyond drawing and painting, as students learn digital animation and demonstrate proficiency in Adobe Illustrator and Photoshop. They use apps like Flipagram to create videos, Book Creator to create iBooks, and Paper by FiftyThree to draw and paint.

In addition to their successful learning spaces and programs, the district has established public and private partnerships with companies and groups like On Hand Schools, Apple, and the Claude Worthington Benedum Foundation, which has propelled the district forward. Rocco also established a powerful partnership with Don Marinelli at Carnegie Mellon University's (CMU) Entertainment Technology Center (ETC, **http://www.etc.cmu.edu**). The center collaborated with the district as they developed a classroom space and a series of courses focused on gaming. The ETC also created educational games for the SMALLab (Situated Multimedia Arts Learning Lab) in the district's middle school. The lab includes an open space with a large floor mat where images are projected. Students engage in embodied learning experiences by grabbing a wand with sensors and interacting with different games. The sensors pick up on the movement of the wands, making the learning interactive. Graduate students from ETC have collaborated with teachers from the school district to design games on topics that students struggle with, like elapsed time and components of grammar. Elizabeth Forward is one of seven local districts with a SMALLab. District leaders were central in creating a SMALLab consortium among the schools to share ideas and resources.

Entertainment Technology Center

The middle school also features an *Energy Lab*. Funded in part by Chevron and in collaboration with the ETC, the lab is a space within the school where students are able to use new technologies to better understand concepts in science and social studies. Graduate students from CMU built an interactive dome that allows students to investigate maps, explore the solar system, and watch interactive videos. Students can manipulate the panels to learn about solar

Elizabeth Forward SMALLab

CMU connects with educators in area school districts to develop relevant technologies through various programs. Two major departments are responsible for collaborating with schools and growing innovative projects.

Community Robotics, Education, and Technology Empowerment, better known as the CREATE Lab, was established to improve the ways that universities connect with the community. They have worked with schools to develop the Arts and Bots program to connect art and robotics for students in elementary and middle school. The CREATE Lab also provides workshops and other events. Other innovative projects have come out of the CREATE Lab, including the Children's Innovation Project and Bird Brain Technologies (developer of the Hummingbird Robotics Kit). The Entertainment Technology Center (ETC) is another collaborative organization out of CMU. This graduate program offered at CMU requires students to work in the community developing games for hospitals, museums, and schools.

energy. In addition to the dome, the lab also has an augmented reality sandbox. The tool uses a motion-sensing input device, called Kinect, and a personal computer to read the contours of the sand, which then projects a three-dimensional image. The sandbox helps students learn about geology and landforms. Through this technology, students can demonstrate ways that land can be divided to create watersheds and tributaries. The Energy Lab is still in development, with additional components being added soon.

Obstacles

Like many other districts, Elizabeth Forward didn't have lots of money or space to build new programs. "We've just niched out little areas," Todd Keruskin said during a March 2015 school tour. The district repurposed their industrial arts space into their Fab Lab. Empty classrooms became learning lounges. Repeated throughout the district tour: If you have enough money to spend on paint, you can do this stuff!

Growing Ideas

"It has changed the culture of our school and our community," Superintendent Rocco explained during that same 2015 tour. The district has strong programs and facilities to support the needs of their intermediate and secondary students. They are now working on additional ways to roll this out to students in their four K–4 schools. District leaders are pursuing funding toward a mobile Fab Lab that will travel to each elementary school for nine weeks. Here, students will have access to 3-D printers, laser cutters, CNC routers, and microcontrollers such as Arduino and Raspberry Pi. With a RV already donated, the district is looking to supply the mobile lab with the latest technologies and hands-on learning tools so that students are able to build skills prior to entering fifth grade. With a one-to-one initiative already happening in the elementary schools, students are building their repertoires with regard to which apps are best for their iPads.

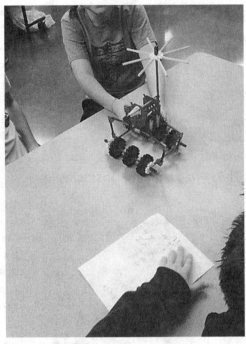

Kiski Robotics

KISKI INTERMEDIATE: BUILDING A SCHOOL FROM THE GROUND UP

Not many school leaders get the opportunity to open a new school building from scratch. In the Kiski Area School District, principal Josh Weaver stepped into a unique position. He was given the opportunity to serve as a building leader a year before the building was actually opened. In that year, he had the ability to plan for the reorganization of an intermediate school. With 600 students in a building for fifth- and sixth-grade students, the school is organized into "families," with a cluster of four classrooms with one teacher for math, reading, science, and humanities.

Fortunate to start a year prior to the opening of the school year, Weaver had the chance to plan with teachers; multiple committees were formed to rewrite the curriculum, talk about school culture, and plan for community outreach. Embedded within the school schedule, students have differentiated flextime. This block of time allows students to pursue special interests and projects. Students can choose to learn about anything from robotics to environmental literacy. During this time, you might see three students building a roller coaster, while three are researching on iPads. One outdoor option for students incorporates a partnership with the Pennsylvania Game Commission and a local fishing shop. The school has a trout tank where students can observe and document the fish but also learn from experts in the field. Weaver explained, "Departmentalized education drives me crazy" (personal communication, February 2015). He envisions an integrated approach, blending subject areas.

With a new school configuration and a focus on STEM, Weaver knew that this was a vast change for parents. He invited them in and got parents involved. Weaver isn't the only one orchestrating this work; the school is lucky to have

Kiski Programming Obstacles

Kiski Outdoor Learning

STEMisphere

a STEM specialist to facilitate learning. The specialist plans and implements all the professional development, pushes into classrooms, and pursues grants.

Outside of the STEM classes, teachers are expected to do at least one unit each year. Teams of teachers designed lessons in engineering, robotics, and programming. Students designed and programmed vehicles to move through a course designed using cereal boxes (see picture).

In order to move the program forward, the district applied to participate in the STEM Excellence Pathway program. Dozens of school districts have worked with the Carnegie Science Center of Pittsburgh to improve their STEM programs. The STEM Excellence Pathway takes schools through an assessment process that includes a self-evaluation, the creation of a plan, identification of resources, and implementation (**http://stemisphere.org/educators**). As a participating school, Kiski has created a sustainable plan to continue to move the school in the right direction.

Obstacles

The school has received several small grants as well as a larger grant from First Energy, but school initiatives are mostly district funded. "Ultimately, we are looking for long-term partnerships. We want to connect with our community as well as other educators doing the same work," stated Weaver (personal communication, February 2015). Finding committed partners has been a challenge for Weaver. As a new principal, he is building his network in an effort to create a group of collaborators to help grow the programs at Kiski. One group that is organizing in his area is the Alle-Kiski Best Practices Collaborative. As a CREATE Lab Satellite Hub, the group is hosting regional professional development for teachers and collaborating on programming for students.

Growing Ideas

STEM summer camps will be offered in the district, including app development and a workshop on designing, making, and marketing cosmetics.

STEAM and making may be new concepts to parents. Here are a few ways to build their knowledge while investing in the home and school connection:

- Send home information about STEAM Making, including relevant research and educational articles.

- Post pictures and videos on your website so that parents can see what STEAM Making looks like in the classroom.

- Ask for volunteers for upcoming projects. Trying sewing for the first time? Don't go at it alone! A few extra sets of hands, especially ones that know how to thread a needle, can really help.

- Host a "Night of Making" so that parents can engage in hands-on learning for themselves.

Support from Engineering is Elementary and an active PTA are important components as Kiski Intermediate moves forward.

INNOVATIVE THINKING: SOUTH FAYETTE SCHOOL DISTRICT

The South Fayette School District is the fastest growing district (by percentage) in Pennsylvania. They are adding about 130 students each year, according to superintendent Bille Rondinelli. The district's emphasis isn't on STEM, STEAM, or making necessarily. Their philosophy is that computational thinking is the new literacy. Simply put, computational thinking is the process of formulating problems and generating solutions. It often includes designing systems and thinking in mathematical ways.

Carnegie Mellon University

Carnegie Mellon University's Center for Computational Thinking is not only building a foundation of research in this area but also providing seminars and other resources (**http://www.cs.cmu .edu/~CompThink**).

CMU
Computational
Thinking

From the district perspective, the definition of computational thinking includes three primary components: problem solving, career vision, and the Habits of Mind. They are working to embed these practices in Grades K–12. The shift to this type of teaching and learning started about four years ago with connected learning that happened after school. They used these programs as *incubator projects*, testing ideas out first. Many ideas started out as after-school clubs working with a small number of students. The clubs are used as a way to pilot programs, gauging student interest, teacher involvement, and overall effectiveness. When ideas are explored this way, the district is able to collect information and determine the program's potential before it is moved formally into the general curriculum.

An early incubator project in the district was the use of Scratch. Initially introduced several years ago as an after-school program for middle school students, the success of this endeavor allowed the district to determine the best fit for their students. The use of Scratch was pushed down through the grades until the district decided to place it in the third-grade curriculum, where it is now taught through the district's STEAM classes.

> When you start students as early as kindergarten, they have a whole new idea of what computer programming means.

A Curriculum for Computational Thinking

Students in the primary grades start with physical coding to develop the vocabulary that will stretch throughout the next twelve years. They use directional words, helping their peers through a maze or from one point in the room to another. This physical coding begins to transfer to programming, as students use Bee Bots (**https://www.bee-bot.us**). These small robots are just right for primary students, teaching sequencing, estimation, and problem solving in a fun way. Students program their bees to go through a maze using simple commands. Students in Grades 1 and 2 also use Scratch Jr., a free app version of MIT's original program but at a more basic level for primary students. They also introduce Lego WeDo at this level, in order to give students more exposure to block-based code.

Bee Bot

In second grade, students begin to write the block-based code on sentence strips then translate it into words. They discuss how these are the same and how are they different during weekly STEAM classes. The introduction to block-based code in the primary grades helps students as they move into the intermediate school.

Vex Robotics

In Grades 3 through 5, students begin using Vex IQ Robotics (**http://www.vexrobotics.com/vexiq**). The district used funding from Digital Promise to purchase the robotic kits. The Vex IQ curriculum includes an online component that allows students to learn the content before doing the physical building. Students complete units on simple machines, motion, mechanisms, and chain reactions, then build and program the robots.

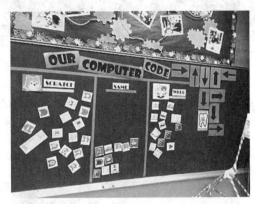
Coding Bulletin Board

In addition to robotics, students are also learning through other STEAM Making tools. Students in fourth grade use Arduino to design shirts for an e-textiles workshop. Second graders use Makey Makey to play music in STEAM class. But the learning in South Fayette isn't contained inside the walls of the building. The district is also growing its environmental literacy program. The school boasts a rooftop garden that serves as an outdoor classroom. Students learn and observe as well as tend to the plants. Their work in gardening doesn't stop there, as one of their STEAM labs (they have one for each grade level in the elementary grades) includes equipment for a hydroponic garden. Growing lettuce and other vegetables has been embedded in the curriculum. See the box on the next page for great resources on hydroponic gardening in schools.

Vex Robotics Construction

Reaching Out

The district has also taken steps to broaden its impact and support other educators in STEAM Making. At the high school level, students have partnered with other school districts to increase knowledge in technology and engineering. One student created a course to teach programming using Python. Not only did the student teach the course to his peers, but a partnership was created so that the content could be shared with two other area school districts.

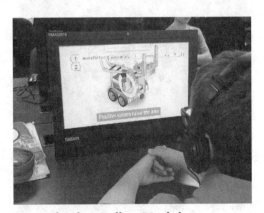
Vex Robotics Online Module

South Fayette also worked with Manchester Academic Charter School to try to duplicate their programming in a different setting. The two schools collaborated on STEAM Making learning units over the course of a semester. "Game Jam" was the culmination of the project, where both schools got together to develop Rube Goldberg devices that went from the physical to the virtual world.

Hydroponic Resources

Kids Gardening	http://www.kidsgardening.org/node/3760	Kids Gardening
Bright Agrotech	http://blog.brightagrotech.com/teaching-hydroponics-in-the-classroom	Bright Agrotech
Boswyck Farms	http://www.boswyckfarms.org/wp-content/uploads/2013/12/Boswyck-Farms-STEM-Education-through-Hydroponics2.pdf	Boswyck Farms
Grow Up Hydro Garden	http://www.growuphydrogarden.com/blog/hydroponics-schools	Grow Up Hydro Garden

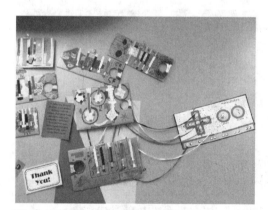

Makey Makey Bulletin Board

Creating for Social Good

The district emphasizes creating for a purpose and working for social good. This philosophy is infused throughout the work done in South Fayette. High school students recently designed a water table to be used with kindergarten students, as they play and learn about simple machines. The inventors have shared their designs at conferences and workshops throughout the region as well. Another team of students have been working on a pen-based flashcard app that can be used by students of all ages. An additional group designed an app called BusBudE for elementary students. Each child is assigned a lanyard with a barcode on it for their backpack. When students get on or off the bus they scan it on a tablet at the front of the bus. A text is then sent to the parent letting them know their child is safe. The team also had the opportunity to work with MAYA Design (http://maya.com), where designers gave the students feedback on the strengths and next steps for the app.

Obstacles

As technology and innovation are rapidly changing, schools can't keep the pace. While South Fayette is doing a pretty good job of maintaining the momentum, they did overcome some obstacles to get people in place to facilitate these programs. Over the course of the last three years, the district saw an increasing need for STEAM leadership. Carefully carving out money from their budget, South Fayette added a tech literacy teacher and a designated STEAM teacher in their

littleBits

schools. They run three 45-minute classes with each homeroom every six days. Currently, the work is isolated to the STEAM labs; teachers are starting to take the learning out into the regular classrooms.

Growing Ideas

With a growing population and increasing enrollment, the district has explored ways to create the type of learning that they want for students. In the middle school, they have decided to abandon the existing computer labs and instead plan to create three learning hubs. Each one will serve as a makerspace with a different focus: graphics and screen printing, prototyping, and a fabrication lab.

The Environmental Discovery Garden is also in process on campus. An outdoor space shared by students in the K–2 and three to five schools will soon be a space where students can study plants and insects but also enjoy the outdoors: reading, writing and reciting poetry, and collaborating with peers. The shared space will allow the district to expand its environmental literacy program to K–12.

SUMMARY

In this chapter, you heard about some innovative school districts building curriculum and programming that is relevant to their students, while also giving them opportunities to develop future-facing dispositions. The Ellis School, Elizabeth Forward, Kiski Area, and South Fayette are embracing opportunities to build amazing opportunities for kids. While each school or district took a different approach, each one is finding success. Perhaps you will take a little bit from each example when you create your own STEAM Making initiative in your school. Building a program and developing a culture that supports STEAM Making takes time. With strong leadership, these organizations have been able to create their own path to creativity and innovation.

What types of out of school learning opportunities do my students engage in? How can this be developed in my school or community?

_____
_____
_____
_____
_____
_____
_____
_____
_____

How might environmental literacy become a part of my school curriculum? What outdoor spaces could facilitate student learning?

_____
_____
_____
_____
_____
_____
_____
_____
_____

CHAPTER 6

Network

Collaboration allows teachers to capture each other's fund of collective intelligence.

—Mike Schmoker

C an STEAM and making occur within one classroom or one school? Sure, but the powerful impact is magnified when educators connect with others in their community. The connection between schools and communities are critical to the success of the STEAM Making initiative. Involvement from libraries, museums, businesses, and other organizations can help to facilitate learning for young people. The learning pathways that may begin in school can be supported and expanded through a network that extends beyond the school building. Nina Barbuto, director of Assemble, articulates this idea well. "Bring in the artists, engineers, and nerds. Schools shouldn't just be stand-alone spaces. They are community hubs. They are the 'churches' of learning" (personal communication, 2015). Figure 6.1 shows schools at the center of the learning ecosystem with the informal learning environments as extensions of formal learning.

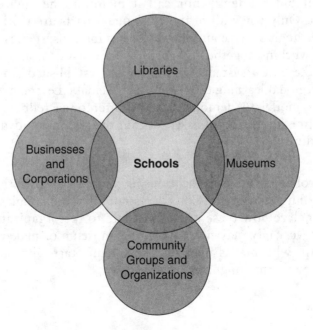

FIGURE 6.1 STEAM Maker Learning Network

REMAKE LEARNING

In 2007, a group of Pittsburgh community leaders came together through the guidance of the Grable Foundation to discuss ways their organizations might collaborate to bring about positive change to the way people live, learn, and play in Pittsburgh. The group, made up of educators, artists, researchers, and librarians adopted the name Kids + Creativity Network. The group met regularly to share ideas and develop initiatives to impact the region. In 2011, Sprout joined the group with a goal to create sustainability and build the capacity of the members through financial support and mentorship.

The Sprout Fund embraces their role in this network as a steward. President and cofounder Cathy Lewis Long summarizes their work in three words: catalyst, convener, and communicator. Sprout is a catalyst for new learning initiatives. The organization brings people together, sponsoring meet-ups and affinity groups all over the city. They work to link organizations and generate partnerships that will mobilize people into action. The network, now called Remake Learning, is literally doing just that. It is remaking what learning can mean for young people. As an organization, Remake Learning is an ecosystem of interconnected schools and groups that are working together to propel this work forward.

A LEARNING ECOSYSTEM

Just as in a scientific ecological system, no one organism has the ability to sustain itself independently nor can it maintain the environment that surrounds it. Only when all of the component parts are working together can the individuals survive and thrive. A learning ecosystem is no different. Individuals working together to nurture the ecosystem and help it grow strengthen the entire system. Pittsburgh has established a network that supports a regional learning ecosystem. The Remake Learning Network has developed a model to demonstrate the interconnectedness of learning centers and the leveraging of assets within the region to advance learning and innovation.

There are probably dozens of locations in your city or town that are a part of your learning ecosystem. Consider some of the examples within this book and analyze how these might translate to the organizations in your area. While every city may not have an art museum or makerspace, begin to brainstorm who makes up your ecosystem. Start with some of these places and spaces that might be in your town.

Five Elements of a Learning Ecosystem

1. **Formal and Informal Learning Environments.** One element that makes Pittsburgh a learning ecosystem is the range of opportunities to learn in both formal and informal ways. Schools pursue connections with local organizations. Many out-of-school programs are thriving, as they provide innovative opportunities within their communities.

2. **Research and Development.** Pittsburgh's colleges and universities are home to scientists, inventors, roboticists, and engineers. They represent educators pushing creativity and innovation.

3. **Advocacy.** Institutions of higher education are researching cutting edge topics in learning and innovation, while also serving as advocates for others in the field of education.

4. **Entrepreneurial Spirit.** A supportive network in Pittsburgh fosters bringing new innovations in technology to the market. Entrepreneurs are creating start-ups at an increasing rate, showing that new ideas and businesses are valued.

5. **Strategic Stewardship.** A part of the learning ecosystem is those that propel ideas forward. Stewardship requires commitment toward a collective vision and the leadership to facilitate others toward that vision. (Remake Learning Playbook, 2015)

Places and Spaces

Library	Science center
University	Museums
Zoo	Aquarium
Home improvement stores	Art gallery
Farm	Greenhouse
Nature center	DIY art shop

Don't forget the number of small businesses or large corporations that might be willing to partner with your educational organization or school district!

GRASSROOTS INNOVATION:
MILLVALE COMMUNITY LIBRARY

Libraries, once stately institutions of knowledge (where you might be shushed by a librarian) are now busy places where knowledge doesn't just come from the books. School and community libraries are booming with innovative programs. Librarians are transforming their once solemn spaces into colorful centers for STEAM Making. But libraries aren't the only organizations supporting a learning ecosystem. Educational partners, community groups, and nonprofit organizations are also exploring ways to support young people in out-of-school (OOS) learning environments.

In researching for this book, I called upon my personal learning network to connect with other educators doing STEAM Making work around the region. Almost every person that I spoke with said, "You have to talk to someone at the Millvale Library!" This community was faced with devastating floods, which wiped out many of its local shops and businesses. With many empty lots and vacant storefronts, many people gave up on the community. In 2013, a group of community members aimed to generate something positive and proactive for the neighborhood. The group put up signs: "Come and meet: Let's make a library!" This was the epitome of real grassroots work. The idea spread mostly by word of mouth, generating more and more interest.

A leadership team assembled and wrote to fifteen different foundations looking for funding. They all said no. The Grable Foundation (responsible for providing seed money to start so many wonderful projects in this book) said yes! While it didn't fund the entire project, it gave the group some seed money to get started. It purchased a property in the once-declining neighborhood. With office space and an apartment upstairs, the building has now been developed into a library and learning space that is revolutionizing a small community.

It took over 50,000 volunteer hours to renovate and modernize the space. Community members shared their expertise as carpenters, welders, plumbers, and so forth. As the building began to take shape, the leadership team started to think about programming. In their first summer, they enlisted support from the Maker Education Initiative and had Maker Corps members run summer programming for kids, including classes and workshops that focused on STEAM Making for young people in the community.

The program was a huge success! One group of students did a puppet show. Working together, they built the stage, made curtains, puppets, and wrote the show. Not only did the kids learn how to create things, but they also hacked things, learning from the deconstruction. "Take apart Tuesdays" became a popular event at the library during the first summer. Kids came in to take apart bikes, learn about the mechanics, and fix the gears. One group took apart a bike and welded it into a working unicycle! One innovative group tried to make a blender bicycle. Although they never got it working, they learned a lot through the process.

With help from MEI, the library continued to develop new ideas and programs to support the young people in Millvale. Fiber Fridays were another busy day at the library, as they hosted an all-girls sewing circle. Another group of teens built a foosball table from found materials using action figures and broom handles. With initial success, library leadership added an after-school program for kids from 3 to 6 p.m., offering workshops to build skills in woodworking and fiber arts. The library has continued to grow with more and more programs being offered. The building is now a centerpiece for a revived community.

Obstacles

One of the obstacles that Millvale faced was the culture. Society doesn't always value manual laborers, but the leadership team celebrated those talents. The library welcomed in carpenters and contractors to help with the initial library renovations. They embraced welders and mechanics to mentor teens. While it might have seemed like an obstacle, the attitude of the community shifted to making the library a success. All individuals contributed in whatever way they could to make the space a central part of the community.

Growing Ideas

Weekly programming is growing in Millvale. The schedule boasts a variety of opportunities to engage in STEAM Making.

- On "Tinker Tuesdays" the community is invited into the library to become an official "Millvale Maker." The library provides the time and the tools for community members to engage in design challenges and try out new tools. Game making, circuitry, and woodworking are popular sessions.

- "Out in the Wild Wednesdays" allow library patrons to engage in making outdoors, exploring through gardening, conservation projects, and games.

- "Maker Thursdays" focus on larger-scale collaborative projects. Wearable technology, carpentry, and recyclable art are explored with library staff.

- "Fiber Fridays" provide the chance to learn how to sew, weave, and create with fiber.

STEAM Maker Starter

Lesson: Tinker and Take Apart

Goal: Explore the ins and outs of items through deconstruction

Timeframe: As long as it takes

Possible Materials: Small appliances and old electronics (many items such as coffee pots, radios, cell phones, computer hard drives, sewing machines, and electronic toys can be donated by students, families, and community businesses), safety goggles, and hand tools

Procedures: Allow students to work individually or in teams to deconstruct their choice of items. Students should use safety precautions as they take apart items. Discovering the interworking of small appliances and electronics will be an exciting experience for students. (You may want to record their reactions as they take things apart.) As they explore the insides of their item, they will discover how things work and how components are connected. They will likely have lots of questions about what they see. Choose a way to capture their wonderings—put them on the board, on sticky notes, or in a student journal.

Deconstruction is a great activity to satisfy student curiosity, but it can also be a springboard for other experiences. Deconstructed electronics can become interesting art pieces or the foundation for a new invention. Some students may also want to see if they can take some completely apart and then back together again!

Reflection: What surprised you about the deconstruction of a _____? What did you find inside? What connections can you make with your existing knowledge in science and math (circuitry, magnetism, programming, etc.)?

INNOVATIVE CONNECTOR: ASSEMBLE

Nina Barbuto started Assemble in 2011 with the goal of connecting artists, technologists, and makers with learners of all ages. Assemble hosts workshops, community events, and interactive gallery shows focused on STEAM principles. With a background in architecture, Barbuto found the connection between STEAM and making while working with kids in south central Los Angeles. For her, architecture was the true connection of science, technology, engineering, art, and math. She sees STEAM and making as very connected. While STEAM is often more associated with the school setting, making is more associated with DIY. Barbuto describes making as "more of a rebellious spirit. Making might seem less mainstream and more punk rock."

> These are all just terms that we use to define activated learning experiences that propel people to explore, engage, wonder, and challenge the existing system to make it better or continue our human evolution.
>
> —Nina Barbuto

Assemble also offers learning parties and open learning times for young people. One popular activity are Saturday *crafternoons*. These weekend sessions promote hands-on learning for young people in Grades 1 through 8. Workshops are free and are led by local makers and community partners. Activities involve collaboration, while fostering connections between friends and neighbors.

Learning experiences at Assemble are meant to empower youth to be confident makers. As young people develop a love of DIY projects, it is the hope that it will also foster an interest in their community and city. One Saturday, community members visited Assemble to create wooden birdfeeders. Kids also created wooden signs using the laser cutter to label the Kincaid St. Garden. Giving back to the community is a huge part of the work at Assemble.

Barbuto says, "We use STEAM Making to help kids find their own agency in the community" (personal communication, May 2015). She described a project where young girls identified a problem in their community and wanted to fix it. With the Nelson Mandela Peace Park dark each night, they decided to create a lighting system to increase neighborhood safety. Through the Tinker Squad program, they built a model of their park and programmed LED lights using the Hummingbird Robotics kit.

ALLEGHENY INTERMEDIATE UNIT: LEARNING HUB FOR STEAM MAKERS

In Pennsylvania, twenty-nine intermediate units serve local school districts to provide collaboration, leverage partnerships, and provide resources. This

Creating community connections is a meaningful way to enhance a STEAM Making program, but not all connections need to be in person. With the use of technology, students can truly connect with anyone around the world. This is true in the connection that Crafton Elementary teacher Susan Kosko made with a boat captain, 1200 miles away from Pittsburgh. As a reading specialist, Mrs. Kosko was used to working intensively with small groups of students who struggled in reading. Her extensive training led her to develop a very effective program, incorporating phonics, phonemic awareness, vocabulary, fluency, and comprehension, but it lacked one component—student interest. The students were not interested in the bland stories and repetitive tasks. They weren't motivated to read in class or at home. Susan eventually hit a frustration point where she knew things had to change. The school year ended and her summer goal was to come back refreshed and with a new plan of attack. Her annual family vacation to Marco Island, Florida, sparked an idea that would change her teaching forever.

The family decided to go on a dolphin watch trip. Susan talked with the friendly captain and crew. Little did she know, she was initiating a relationship that would impact her students back in Pittsburgh for years to come. She began regular Skype sessions with the Dolphin Explorer team. Susan planned vocabulary around the Skype topics and used research to engage her students. Her classes loved connecting with Captain Chris and James, who were new to working with elementary school students. Together, Susan and the Florida team collaborated on lessons, including the use of LiveStream clips. Susan's lessons developed student vocabulary and comprehension prior to the Skype sessions. Student motivation began to climb. Students were asking for more things to read about dolphins. They were *actually* doing their homework! As the connection with the Dolphin Project continued, students also began to develop empathy. They wrote about ways to save dolphins and started a fundraiser to collect money for injured dolphins. The experience culminated as the students were able to Skype live as a dolphin rescue took place. The amazing recovery of the creature was eventually featured on ABC's Saturday morning show, Sea Rescue. The students were also featured on the show because of their ongoing involvement with the Dolphin Project.

The connection to Marco Island has continued as students connect with the Dolphin Explorer team regularly. More and more classes across the country are also connecting. Check out their website to see how your students might benefit from this global connection (**http://dolphin-study.com**).

Dolphin Explorer

broad range of services includes curriculum development, instructional coaching, educational planning, technical assistance, pupil personnel services, and professional development. The Allegheny Intermediate Unit (AIU3) serves forty-two school districts in Allegheny County. While their primary function is to provide services and act as a liaison, AIU3 goes beyond this role. In 2013, they established the transformED space, which is a digital playground for educational networking and learning. Check out their video for more details (**https://vimeo .com/59037421**).

transformED

transformED is an area with the AIU3 facility to support school districts' efforts to explore new technologies including Gigapan, 3-D printers, and Hummingbird Robotics. It is also a space to collaborate and plan innovative programs. The collaborative space offers creative sessions for teachers to explore new teaching tools, allowing them to integrate new strategies into their practice. In 2014, they also developed the Center for Creativity within their teaching and learning departments. Closely connected to the Remake Learning Network, the Center for Creativity serves as a regional hub for resources and professional development for teachers and administrators.

Conversation With Jesse Schell

One of the components that can enhance a STEAM and making program is outreach. Thinking beyond the school walls can bring unexpected opportunities for teachers and students. This outreach can come through neighborhood businesses, corporate partners, or grant foundations.

For many young people, it is the dream job. Jesse Schell, owner of gaming company Schell Games, designs video games for a living. He and his team have even designed for Disney. The company values education and partners with schools in many ways. Schell personally reaches out to local school districts to talk about creativity and innovation. He visited Crafton Elementary during the STEAM Showcase of Learning and presented to students and parents about his work. He discussed the possible career paths with students. He believes that kids are interested in the notion of creative careers. Schell Games has worked with Elizabeth Forward teaching students the basics of video game design. Schell Games has also been working with the Pittsburgh Children's Museums "play-testing" a game with three- to five-year-olds featuring Daniel Tiger from Mr. Rogers' Neighborhood.

The Schell Games team visits lots of schools to play test games. This is an awesome experience for kids, as the team tells them that they want student feedback and that *their* opinion matters. It may even change the course of a game! The Schell Games team visited Crafton Elementary a few times. The students were given iPads with a preloaded game. The students were instructed

(Continued)

(Continued)

to play for 30 minutes, trying not to talk to their peers. While it was hard for them to contain their excitement at first, the students became hyper-focused as they explored the fantasy-themed game focusing on improving student vocabulary. Just as much as the students were enthusiastic, so were the team members from Schell Games. They were interested in understanding what students liked about the game as well as the kinks that students found. Schell Games continued to visit over the course of a year and a half as the game was revised and improved. Through the experience, students learned an important lesson in their own design as well. With the repeated feedback on the game, students were able to see how long it actually takes to complete the design of a game and get it out on the market.

West Liberty Marble Run

EXPANDING THE NETWORK: HIGHER EDUCATION

Colleges and universities are joining in the Maker Movement and embracing STEAM education as well. They are adding courses and programs in response to the call for STEM and STEAM education. Some are partnering with school districts in unique ways. One has even created a makerspace so that undergraduate education majors are learning the skills they will need to student teach and eventually enter the workforce.

The Center for Arts and Education at West Liberty University

Think back to your undergraduate experience. If you took any elementary education courses, you were likely asked to complete a variety of projects from lesson plans, to mock children's books, to posters, and physical models. Now imagine if there had been a place on campus where you could not only find a plethora of materials to do these projects but also someone who might be able to provide you with some guidance or hands-on expertise to help you do it. West Liberty University has taken the idea of a maker space and designed an amazing place for education majors and others to tinker and learn. This brightly colored room used to be the business office. It now holds woodworking tools, relevant technology, recyclable items, and every piece of crafting supplies you could ever imagine.

Lou Karas, director of the center, explains that it is a place where students come to do projects for their classes while others just come to hang out.

They study or talk, because it is a space that is different. Colorful artwork covers the walls. Bold IKEA furniture creates areas for small group work. One wall is set up with a pegboard that students have turned into a marble run experiment. We know that it is not the space that makes makers, but this new center helped to develop the maker mindset on a once traditional college campus.

When I visit on a mild January day, I think back to my undergraduate experience. I can recall a dozen times that I had to call home to ask for money to buy craft supplies, stickers, construction paper, and so forth, to fund a project for a class in children's literature or methods in elementary art. What a difference this space would have made!

Students from the neighboring College of Science visited for a chemistry class when they built combustion models. They used soldering irons, wire strippers, and glass cutters. A class of special education majors studying the TEACCH model visited the center to make task boxes. The students designed sorting activities and sensory games, all out of materials from the center. Lou sadly explained that one student still insisted on color printing materials from Pinterest and laminating them all for her project—guess you can't win them all!

Through generous funding from the Benedum Foundation, the center has a bunch of tools for students to use. They have a dozen Giga Pan Kits, Hummingbird robots, Makey Makeys, and littleBits. Karas explains that the Giga Pan is actually a requirement in the College of Education. She talks with students about ways to incorporate new tools into their instruction.

One common undergrad assignment is the development of a personal philosophy of education. I'm sure we all recall drafting a paper to describe our beliefs about education. Rather than a traditional approach, WLU students used materials from the center to capture their philosophy in hand-made books and shadow boxes. While the content of the assignment stayed the same, now students are able to show their understanding in different ways.

Another assignment transformation included the task of writing a story about an everyday hero. Traditionally this project would have been an essay. Instead, students were asked to write the story and screen print a poster. Students visited the center to learn how to use the screen printer and then designed their print. The new prints were presented along with their written work.

The undergraduate program at WLU has a focus on immersion in local schools, combined with relevant professional development in STEAM Making. For example, students may spend Wednesdays at the Wheeling

Country Day School for ELA instruction and Tuesdays and Thursdays doing math and science instruction at Wheeling Elementary. On Fridays, students spend time at the center doing professional development with Karas. She stresses the importance of giving them exposure to real programs that they will use in the field. This semester students learned about Touch Math and Handwriting without Tears. Students also benefit from workshops in bookmaking, puppetry, and screen printing. The sessions allow students to further prepare for their work after college.

West Liberty Storage

Each summer, WLU also offers professional development to preservice and active teachers. (Last year, they had teachers from three states!) The week-long course attracts music teachers, band directors, visual arts teachers, and elementary, middle school, and high school content teachers. They meet to learn about graphic design and the use of the Hummingbird Robotics Kit through the lens of art, engineering, and other disciplines. The workshop is also connected to the CREATE Lab Arts & Bots Project.

Career Connector: Robert Morris University

In 2015, Robert Morris University (RMU) joined with several area school districts to form the Ohio River Consortium. The partnership is designed to increase project-based learning in elementary and middle schools. With grant funding from the Grable Foundation, the participating districts will create makerspaces in the elementary schools in Year 1 and in all middle schools by Year 2. The schools will also host preservice teachers and share professional development.

RMU works closely with Avonworth Elementary to support their ventures in making. Teachers have visited the university, presenting to undergraduates in their science methods courses. In turn, the RMU students have volunteered in the elementary school. The collaboration was critical to the development of *Maker Madness*. This day-long event involves parents and RMU undergrads working at making stations to engage students in activities of their choice.

Principal Scott Miller used a checklist for students to choose their activities for the event. This allowed undergrads to plan challenges and building projects for students. Students selected from the options in Figure 6.2.

Favorite Activity (1X)	Other Choices (2X)	Maker Madness Stations
		Sewing
		Weaving
		Tool exploration
		Build it
		Circuit blocks
		Recycled art—group building
		Recycled art—individual building
		Recycled art—design challenge

FIGURE 6.2   Maker Madness Student Survey

SUMMARY

The connections that can be created to STEAM and making are endless. This chapter shared a few of the innovators within the network in Pittsburgh. Libraries, educational agencies, colleges, and universities are a part of the learning ecosystem that makes STEAM Making a successful approach to learning. As you explore the learning network in your region, you may find that STEAM Making may already be alive and well. Reach out to your community and find out!

List the local colleges and universities near your school/district:

_____

_____

_____

_____

_____

_____

_____

_____

_____

Brainstorm a list of the groups, organizations, and people in your school community that could support your STEAM Making journey:

_____

_____

_____

_____

_____

_____

_____

_____

_____

_____

CHAPTER 7

StArt

As you read through the previous chapters, you may have been struck by various examples. Stories may have spurred ideas or ways to implement STEAM Making in your school. This final chapter will give you some additional direction for how to start.

Maybe you are thinking about starting a STEAM Maker club for sewing or woodworking. Maybe you are going to use Scratch to enhance one of your lessons. Maybe you're going to explore hydroponics for your school. Remember it's OK to start small—just start!

So, let's commit to one idea. What is one thing that you will try in your classroom or school?

_____

_____

_____

What will you need to get started?

_____

_____

_____

_____

_____

_____

PLAN FOR STUDENT ENGAGEMENT

I find that when I commit something to writing, it is more likely that I will actually do it. Now that you have written down some preliminary ideas and potential first steps, start mapping out your plan. You may need to connect to local experts, get some materials, or explore funding. These are things that may take time, but don't let that deter you. The reaction from your students and the learning that takes place is undeniable.

During a conversation with one STEAM Maker, he shared his beliefs with me. "Anyone can start making tomorrow." It's all about your ability to facilitate. STEAM Making isn't about following every direction or a certain set of steps. It requires a culture of experimentation. This culture is one that elevates student learning by allowing the students to pursue their individual interests. This maker reminded me that, whether you're making paper airplanes or measuring and cutting wood for a project, the learning is apparent. You can see whether someone is "getting it" or not. I can't think of a better way to assess learning! "Your friends can't see your spelling test, but they can see if you built the tallest, coolest tower," the maker imparted. This transparency is part of what creates the eagerness in children that results in 100% engagement.

CONNECT TO LOCAL EXPERTS

It is likely that there are STEAM Makers in your school, district, neighborhood, or city. Get the word out—post something on Facebook, put it on your website, or in the district newsletter. Ask your colleagues, neighbors, and parents: Who has a skill to share with the students?

Who Are STEAM Makers?		
Hackers	Musicians	Roboticists
Builders	Designers	Mechanics
Librarians	Crafters	Gardeners
Hobbyists	Seamstresses	Scrapbookers
Teachers	Costumers	Entrepreneurs
Scientists	Tinkerers	Inventors
Engineers	Woodworkers	Programmers
Painters	Knitters	Developers
Sculptors	Architects	. . . and more

GET RESOURCES

You will likely need some materials to get started with your STEAM Making idea. You may decide to use recyclable materials or things that you already have available, or you may want to try some tech tools. While either pathway will engage your students, decide what you think will best meet the needs of the kids. The makerspace supply list in Appendix E will probably help. You may also want to consider the Ten Tools to Try in Table 7.1.

TABLE 7.1 Ten Tools to Try

TOOL	PURPOSE	WEBSITE	QR CODE
Lego Mindstorms	Intricate systems combined with technology give students the opportunity to build and program robots.	http://www.lego.com/en-us/mindstorms	Lego Mindstorms
Lego WeDo	Building and programming kits for pre–K through elementary age.	https://education.lego.com/en-us	Lego WeDo
Scratch	Free online tool that allows kids to create games and animations then share them with others.	https://scratch.mit.edu	Scratch
Makey Makey	Explore circuits and create new ways to change your keyboard or create music.	http://www.makeymakey.com	Makey Makey
Snap Circuits	Build circuits to power a fan, ring a bell, or turn on a radio. Snap Circuits also has a "green" kit to create solar and water powered devices.	http://www.snapcircuits.net	Snap Circuits
Arduino	Tinkering by connecting circuit boards and sensors.	https://www.arduino.cc	Arduino
Raspberry Pi	Can connect to Scratch and other tools to learn coding.	https://www.raspberrypi.org/learning/teachers-classroom-guide	Raspberry Pi

(Continued)

Note: It may be helpful to cover other QR codes in this table with a sheet of paper to help focus your phone or tablet on a particular QR code.

TABLE 7.1 (Continued)

TOOL	PURPOSE	WEBSITE	QR CODE
Hummingbird Robotics	Build and program moving robots.	http://www.hummingbirdkit.com	**Hummingbird Robotics**
Sphero	A connected learning toy that builds student knowledge in math content while programming the tool to move.	http://www.sphero.com	**Sphero**
littleBits	Electronic building blocks to develop design thinking and logic.	http://littlebits.cc	**littleBits**

Donors Choose

Since these tools aren't all free, explore available funding sources like Donors Choose (**http://www.donorschoose.org**) and PledgeCents (**https://www.pledgecents.com**). You can post your project ideas and wait for the donations to roll in. You never know who might be interested in funding your innovative project.

GOT GRANTS?

There are lots of grants that are available to jumpstart your project ideas. Table 7.2 has several grants for you to explore, but a simple Google search will turn up dozens more. A small grant may be all you need to start your version of a Light Bulb Lab in your room or to stock your makerspace with

PledgeCents

tools and materials. Writing grants may seem daunting at first, but once you've gathered the basic information for one grant, you may be able to use the same information for other grants. Be sure to follow their template and guidelines but know that you can use some of your grant narrative for multiple applications.

Here are a few steps if you are just getting started:

1. **Search for applicable grants.** Some grants are available only to certain areas, grade levels, or organizations. Be sure to read the requirements carefully before you devote a lot of time preparing your proposal.

2. **Gather your basic information.** Most grants are going to want to know about your school and district demographics. You may want to

generate a paragraph or chart that details how many students are in your class/school/district, general information about the make-up of your area, and the economic status.

3. **Plan your budget.** Funders are looking for a clear and detailed plan that includes a sound budget. Be specific about what you want to do and what exactly the money will be used for.

4. **Be accountable.** How will you measure the effectiveness of what you plan to do? Most grants will require a final report, including some data to show that the program was executed and that you did what you said you were going to do.

Don't be discouraged if you are not funded right away. Keep trying! The more you write grants, the better you will get. Sometimes you may need to revise your initial proposal and resubmit it. Some funders will provide feedback on submissions as well. Most agencies will list previous grant recipients on their websites. Look through the projects that have been funded in the past; this will give you an idea if you are on the right track.

TABLE 7.2 Grant Opportunities

FUNDING SOURCE	AMOUNT	TOPIC
American Honda Foundation	$20,000–$75,000	STEM focus
Lowe's	$2,000–$5,000	Projects with permanence
Crayola	$5,000	Art and innovation
Motorola	$10,000–$60,000	STEM
Westinghouse	$3,000	STEM
SnapDragon Book Foundation	Up to $20,000	Books for school libraries
McCarthey Dressman Education Foundation	Up to $10,000	"Fresh strategies to encourage critical inquiry"
Wallace Foundation	$30,000–$100,000	STEM education
Innovating Worthy Projects Foundation	$1,000–$10,000	Innovative programs
Department of Environmental Protection	$3,000	STEM

(Continued)

TABLE 7.2 (Continued)

FUNDING SOURCE	AMOUNT	TOPIC
Chevron	Unlimited	STEM
Toshiba American Foundation	Up to $5,000	Innovation in math and science classrooms designed by teachers or small teams of teachers for use in their own schools
Grable Foundation	Unlimited	Any
Benedum Foundation	Unlimited	Any—with an emphasis on collaboration with West Virginia

My Two Cents

As I think back to when we started our STEAM Making journey, there are so many things that I know now that I wish I knew then. The biggest thing is probably that we didn't need fancy technology or expensive kits to engage our kids in meaningful STEAM Maker learning. And while the grants were helpful (and so generous) we really could have done this work without them. In the midst of it all, I thought "Ooh, that's cool. We need to buy that." Or "I saw that in someone's library—we need one of those!" When it really comes down to it, it's not about all the bells and whistles. It's about the opportunities, the engagement, and the change in mindset that makes this successful. Kids will design things using cardboard boxes. They can learn programming using free tools. Teachers can shift their practices without pricey professional development or traveling to far-off conferences.

My personal STEAM Maker journey is much like the chapter titles in this book. Initially, I was intrigued by the idea of STEM and STEAM education and took the time to *learn*. This was early on in the STEM push, so the resources that exist now weren't around then, but I read everything I could. I found places that were dabbling in STEM in formal and informal settings and talked with them. I knew if I was going to encourage my teachers to take a risk and try this, then I better know my stuff!

Slowly, I started to *change* my own beliefs about education. I began to see the possibilities in changing learning environments and instructional practices. It was then that I also started to share this new knowledge with my teachers, building their understanding in an effort to keep them current and keep our work relevant.

I *failed*. The first year we had our STEAM studio, it wasn't everything it could have been. I failed to garner teacher buy-in at the level I expected. I failed to promote our work as much as I could have. The most important part of these failures (and so many more) is that I learned from them and tried to develop solutions. Failing doesn't feel good, but I know that without those early hiccups, I would not have pushed myself to get better personally or professionally or devote the time and effort needed to push this initiative forward.

In the years that followed, I worked to build leadership among the teachers, highlighting the STEAM Maker work they were doing in their classrooms, especially showcasing the work that demonstrated meaningful connections with our existing curriculum. As we continued our journey, more information about the Crafton STEAM Studio was promoted throughout our community and across the region. I wrote articles for state and local publications, putting our work on the map. I also encouraged teachers to present their work at educational conferences. (Reading specialist Susan Kosko presented her work at both the state and national level!) The positive PR gave our program more momentum, and more teachers began to get involved, further growing our program. The attention that we brought to our STEAM Maker work propelled us to getting additional funding, because the program had been so successful.

Connect learning. Real-world connections. Connected curriculum. Career connections. When learning is connected to other things, it becomes more meaningful to students. Through our journey, we connected the ideas of STEAM education and the Maker Movement into a new model for learning—STEAM Making. Hopefully the story of Crafton Elementary provides some insight into one possible path to STEAM Making in schools. Our students made some tremendous connections: connections between content areas, connections to their global peers, and connections to the possibilities beyond the school building.

It is exciting to *build* something from nothing. The opportunity to develop a new program was a huge responsibility but one that was challenging and fun. Just as the schools within this book, I enjoyed the physical building. Getting into the STEAM studio at lunch, I loved building K'NEX roller coasters with the fifth-grade girls and earning my hot gluing badge with the lunch crew. The relationships that were built throughout this journey were critical to its success. The building of a STEAM Maker program included many components; after-school programming, lunch-and-learn sessions, professional development, and career talks all contributed to the development of curriculum components as well.

(Continued)

(Continued)

When there is a *network* of people and resources all working toward a common goal, initiatives move forward. I was lucky to be a part of the Remake Learning Network. The opportunity to meet other like-minded school leaders was inspiring. Talking with those outside of formal education opened my eyes up to the possibilities for extending learning pathways out into the community. There are so many people out there who are doing GREAT things! My personal learning network on Twitter has also been a great source of new knowledge as well as affirmation of the importance of STEAM and making for young people.

How do you *start*? Getting started on any new initiative can be a challenge. A STEAM Making program can be as large or small as you want it to be. When we started several years ago, I didn't know where to start either, but I knew we had to start somewhere. Starting small projects and adding new things each year was a helpful approach. Building momentum with teachers happened gradually through small conversations and larger training sessions. Every step contributed to the greater goal of changing our practices. Getting started with STEAM Making was one of the best decisions I ever made—risky at first, but well worth it.

So, is your school ready to make a change and take on the challenges that come with STEAM Making? Review the Readiness Checklist in Table 7.3 to determine where your school, district, or organization is on the continuum. This tool might help to begin the conversation in your school and identify areas of need.

SUMMARY

Education is changing, shifting away from standardization and toward creativity and innovation. We need disruptors—those who are willing to take a chance on practices like STEAM and making because they foster the forward-facing dispositions that we want our students to possess. "I think STEAM makes a lot of sense to folks. No matter what you call you call, it's the same pedagogical approach. It is relevant and allows students to dissect problems" (personal communication, January 2015), Gregg Behr advocates. This approach also makes sense to kids.

It is a critical time in education. We have an opportunity to continue on in the same way that we have in education or begin a journey toward relevant learning. Will Richardson recently opened up a conference by asserting that most kids in our schools don't want to learn more about the stuff they are learning in school. Some educators may take offense to this. Aren't we all trying our best to provide a rigorous curriculum and engaging instruction?

TABLE 7.3 Readiness Checklist

	EXPLORING	IN DEVELOPMENT	ESTABLISHED
VISION			
Our school/district/organization/program uses project-based learning integrated STEAM subjects.	❏	❏	❏
Our school/district/organization/program integrates technology and virtual learning.	❏	❏	❏
LEADERSHIP			
Ongoing professional development has been provided to build capacity for STEAM/Making teaching and learning.	❏	❏	❏
A communicated plan for STEAM/Making or curriculum has been developed.	❏	❏	❏
Teachers/staff members understand the importance of developing programs to support 21st century skills.	❏	❏	❏
COMMUNITY			
Partnerships with businesses and community groups help to extend STEAM/Making experiences outside of school.	❏	❏	❏
PHYSICAL SPACE			
Classrooms/learning spaces are equipped to support project work and collaboration	❏	❏	❏
Areas are designated for STEAM/Making materials, resources, and ongoing projects.	❏	❏	❏
TRAINING AND DEVELOPMENT			
Teachers/staff members have opportunities to reflect on student work and implement new initiatives within their workdays.	❏	❏	❏
Students have regular opportunities to use digital tools like social media, Skype, and blogging to communicate and collaborate with others outside of the school.	❏	❏	❏
Opportunities exist for students to explore STEAM careers.	❏	❏	❏

Maybe we should ask our students:

- What do you want to learn?
- How can you show that you understand?
- What can I do to facilitate that?

What we decide to call it is irrelevant. STEAM or STEM-X, different professionals like different words. At the intersection of STEAM and making, powerful learning occurs—not just for students but for teachers too. Embracing STEAM Making means changing your mindset and your practice. Hopefully, this book provides you with the resources and motivation to get started. Are you ready to be a STEAM Maker?

Appendix A

STEAM Studio Badge System

WOODWORKING

Tools like hammers, saws, screwdrivers, pliers, and clamps are used in woodworking. These can be used in conjunction with wood, nails, screws, glue, and other materials to build models and contraptions.

Show what you know:

- Demonstrate knowledge of tool names and purpose.
- Model appropriate use by

    o Using a saw to cut in a straight line

    o Using the electric drill with care

    o Using goggles and maintaining personal safety

SCRATCH

Scratch can be used to create digital stories, games, and animations.

Show what you know:

- Create a "sprite."
- Program the sprite to walk back and forth, turn and talk, or other motions and actions.
- Add background and other objects to the scene.

X-ACTO KNIFE

The X-ACTO can be used to cut cardboard or other materials.

Show what you know:

- Open and close the knife safely.
- Cut out a shape with care.
- Change a blade.

ANIMATION

Different tools can be used to animate including Movie Maker, PowToons or other websites.

Show what you know:

- Make a picture move.
- Make a flipbook.
- Create a scene.
- Add sounds.
- Use stop-motion animation to create a story.

SEWING

Tools for hand sewing and the sewing machine can be used to create something.

Show what you know:

- Hand sewing
  - Thread a needle.
  - Tie a knot.
  - Sew a button.
- Sewing machine
  - Thread the bobbin.
  - Change the thread.
  - Demonstrate different stitches.
  - Finish a piece.

HOT GLUE GUN

A hot glue gun is a hand tool used to fuse items together using heated glue.

Show what you know:

- Glue something.
- Reload the gun with glue.
- Use materials with safety.
- Let gun cool and clean up.

SOLDERING

A soldering iron is a hand tool used to melt solder so that it can flow into the joint between two pieces of metal.

Show what you know:

- Find a safe area to work.
- Use goggles.
- Wipe at the right time.
- Create three joints.
- Wait to cool.
- Clean up.

Source: Woodworking, Scratch, Animation, and Sewing images courtesy of Dynamic Graphics/ LiquidLibrary/ThinkStock; X-ACTO Knife, Hot Glue Gun, and Soldering images courtesy of clipart.com.

Appendix B
Sample Professional Development Plan

Phase 1   Introduction
            Possible sessions:

> Intro to STEAM and making
>
> Developing the Habits of Mind
>
> Design thinking in the classroom

Phase 2   Skill building
            Possible sessions:

> Stop motion animation
>
> Scratch
>
> 3-D printing
>
> Crafting and building using hand tools
>
> Sewing and weaving

Phase 3   Curriculum
            Possible sessions:

> Using children's literature to support
> hands-on learning
>
> Infusing STEAM and making into the
> content areas
>
> Gaming in the classroom

Phase 4   Reflection
            and assessment
            Possible sessions:

> Intro to badging (digital or physical)
>
> Developing rubrics assess student learning
>
> Journaling to capture student learning
>
> Digital presentations to show your work

Appendix C

English Language Arts Extensions Chart

Extend the story or create a new ending using a digital tool: • Scratch • Movie Maker • Powtoons • Storyboard That	Design a new toy.	Build a recycled art sculpture.
Design an experiment.	Invent a solution to a problem.	Create a 3-D setting.
Build a physical model.	Create a character puppet, figure, or doll.	Design a game (physical or animated).

Appendix D

STEAM Making Permission Slip

Date _____

To Whom It May Concern,

I, _____, give _____
        (Principal/School Leader)   (Teacher)

permission to think outside the box and design instruction that is challeng-

ing and fun for students. _____ is encouraged to
                                                    (Teacher)

collaborate with his/her colleagues to integrate content areas and pursue the

awesome possibilities of STEAM Making in our school.

With enthusiastic support,

_____

Signature

Appendix E

Makerspace Supply List

FREE, RECYCLABLE MATERIALS

- ❑ Plastic
- ❑ Clothespins
- ❑ Binder clips
- ❑ Popsicle sticks
- ❑ Cereal boxes
- ❑ Thread needles
- ❑ Wood blocks/scraps
- ❑ Packing supplies (bubble wrap, packing peanuts)
- ❑ Fabric
- ❑ Egg cartons
- ❑ Foam trays
- ❑ Metal hangers
- ❑ Yarn
- ❑ Toilet paper/towel rolls
- ❑ Broken toys
- ❑ Greeting cards
- ❑ Canisters
- ❑ Wallpaper samples

INEXPENSIVE THINGS TO BUY

- ❑ Buttons
- ❑ Ping pong balls
- ❑ Peg boards
- ❑ Craft items (pipe cleaners, pom poms, etc.)
- ❑ Hot glue guns and glue sticks
- ❑ Button batteries
- ❑ LED lights
- ❑ Small motors (robotics)
- ❑ Brass fasteners
- ❑ Scissors
- ❑ Tape
- ❑ Felt
- ❑ Rubber bands
- ❑ Beads
- ❑ Batteries
- ❑ Wire
- ❑ Goggles
- ❑ Bins/storage
- ❑ Wire cutters

THINGS THAT REQUIRE A BIT OF A BUDGET

- ❑ Hand tools (hammers, saws, screwdrivers, drills)
- ❑ Sewing machines
- ❑ Soldering irons
- ❑ Hummingbird Robotics kits
- ❑ K'NEX
- ❑ Makey Makey
- ❑ Lego Wedo/Mindstorms kits

Appendix F

Websites for STEAM and Making

MAKERSPACES

Assemble

> http://assemblepgh.org

Hack Pittsburgh

> http://www.hackpittsburgh.org

New York Hall of Science

> http://www.nysci.org

Wanger Family Fab Lab at Museum of Science and Industry

> http://www.msichicago.org/whats-here/fab-lab

TechShop

> http://www.techshop.ws

The Exploratorium

> http://www.exploratorium.edu

ENGINEERING AND DESIGN

Engineering is Elementary

> http://www.eie.org

Virginia Children's Engineering Council

> http://www.childrensengineering.org

PBS Design Squad
    http://pbskids.org/designsquad

Discover Engineering
    http://www.discovere.org

The Kennedy Center Art's Edge
    https://artsedge.kennedy-center.org/educators.aspx

SCIENCE

The Buck Institute of Education
    http://bie.org

My Science Box
    http://www.mysciencebox.org

Extreme Science
    http://www.extremescience.com

STEM Works
    http://stem-works.com

Kids Do Ecology
    http://kids.nceas.ucsb.edu/index.html

Kids Ahead
    http://kidsahead.com

CAREERS

CanTeen
    http://canteengirl.org

Career Aisle
    http://knowitall.scetv.org/careeraisle/students/elementary/index.cfm

Engineer Girl
    http://www.engineergirl.org

Appendix G

Student Reflection Sheet

Student name: _____   Group name: _____

What did you create? _____

_____

_____

What does it do? _____

_____

_____

How did your group decide on that? _____

_____

_____

What were the strengths of the group? _____

_____

_____

What would your team do differently next time? _____

_____

_____

What did you contribute to the group? _____

_____

_____

How would you rate your performance on this task?   4   3   2   1

References and Additional Resources

Ash, K. (2012). Digital badges would represent students' skill acquisition: Initiatives seek to give students permanent online records for developing specific skills. *Education Week, 5*(3), 24–25. Retrieved from http://edweek.org/dd/articles/2012/06/13/03badges.h05.html

Beckman, B. (2010). *Awakening the creative spirit: Bringing the arts to spiritual direction.* New York: Church Publishing.

Bevan, B., Petrich, M., & Wilkinson, K. (2015). Tinkering is serious play. *STEM for All, 4*(72), 28–33.

Bevins, S., Carter, K., Jones, V., Moye, J., & Ritz, J. (2012). The technology and engineering educator's role in producing a 21st century workforce. *Technology and Engineering Teacher, 72* (3), 8–12.

Carey, K. (2012). A future full of badges. *The Chronicles of Higher Education.* Retrieved from http://chronicle.com/article/A-Future-Full-of-Badges/131455/

Catterall, J. (2002). The arts and the transfer of learning. In R. J. Deasy (Ed.), *Critical links: Learning in the arts and student academic and social development.* Washington, DC: Arts Education Partnership.

Cengage Learning. (2014). *What students say they need in order to become more engaged in class.* Retrieved from http://assets.cengage.com/pdf/mi_digital_transition.pdf

The Conference Board, Inc., the Partnership for 21st Century Skills, Corporate Voices for Working Families, and the Society for Human Resource Management. (2006). *Are they really ready to work?* Retrieved from http://www.p21.org/storage/documents/FINAL_REPORT_PDF09-29-06.pdf

Coon, R. (2012). *Pittsburgh: Forging a 21st Century Learning community.* Retrieved from Educause Review at http://er.educause.edu/articles/2012/11/pittsburgh-forging-a-21st-century-learning-community

Costa, A., & Kallick, B. (2008). *Learning and leading with Habits of Mind: 16 essential characteristics for success.* Alexandria, VA: Association for Supervision and Curriculum Development.

Dail, W. (2013). On cultural polymathy: How visual thinking, culture, and community create a platform for progress. *The STEAM Journal, 1*(1), article 7.

Dearden, H. (2011). Touching wood. *TCE: The Chemical Engineer* (838), 22–23.

Dweck, C. (2006). *Mindset: The new psychology of success.* New York: Random House.

Dweck, C. (2014). *Carol Dweck: The power of believing that you can improve*, TED Ideas Worth Spreading. Retrieved from https://www.ted.com/talks/carol_dweck_the_power_of_believing_that_you_can_improve?language=en

Eger, J. (2013) STEAM . . . Now! *The STEAM Journal 1*(1). Retrieved from http://scholarship.claremont.edy/steam/vol1/iss1/8

Fleming, L. (2015). Worlds of making: Best practices for establishing a makerspace for your school. *Corwin Connected Educators Series*. Thousand Oaks, CA: Corwin.

Henriksen, D. (2014). Full STEAM ahead: Creativity in excellent STEM teaching practices. *The STEAM Journal, 1*(2), 1–8.

International Technology Education Association (ITEA/ITEEA). (2000). *The standards for technological literacy: Content for the study of technology*. Reston, VA: Author

International Technology Education Association (ITEA/ITEEA). (2002). *The standards for technological literacy: Content for the study of technology*. Reston, VA: Author

International Technology Education Association (ITEA/ITEEA). (2003). *Advancing excellence in technological literacy: Student assessment, professional development, and program standards*. Reston, VA: Author.

International Technology Education Association (ITEA/ITEEA). (2007). *The standards for technological literacy: Content for the study of technology*. Reston, VA: Author.

Kalil, T. (2015, July 8). Inspiring makers in Pittsburgh. [Web log post]. Retrieved from https://www.whitehouse.gov/blog/2015/07/08/inspiring-makers-pittsburgh

Krigman, E. (2014). Gaining STEAM: Teaching science through art. *U.S. News & World Report*. Retrieved from http://www.usnews.com/news/stem-solutions/articles/2014/02/13/gaining-steam-teaching-science-though-art

Lammi, M., & Becker, K. (2013). Engineering design thinking. *Journal of Technology Education, 24*(2), 55–77.

Landau, M., & Chisholm, D. (1995). The arrogance of optimism: Notes on failure-avoidance management. *Journal Of Contingencies & Crisis Management, 3*(2), 67.

Lasky, D., & Yoon, S. A. (2011). Making space for the act of making: Creativity in the engineering design classroom. *Science Educator, 20*(1), 34–43.

Lu, K. (2009). A study of engineering freshman regarding nanotechnology understanding. *Journal of STEM Education, 10*(1 & 2), 7–15.

Martinez, S. L., & Stager, G. (2013). *Invent to learn: Making, tinkering, and engineering in the classroom*. Torrance, CA: Constructing Modern Knowledge Press.

Mishra, P., Terry, C., Henrisken, D., & the Deep-Play Research Group (2013). Square peg, round hole, good engineering. *Tech Trends, 57*(2), 22–25.

Miller, A. (2014, May 20). *PBL and STEAM education: A natural fit*. Retrieved from http://www.edutopia.org/blog/pbl-and-steam-natural-fit-andrew-miller

Morozov, E. (2014, January 13). Making it. *The New Yorker*. Retrieved from http://www.newyorker.com/magazine/2014/01/13/making-it-2

National Academy of Engineering. (2010). *Standards for K–12 Engineering Education?* Washington, DC: The National Academies Press.

National Research Council. (2011). *Successful K–12 STEM education: Identifying effective approaches in science, technology, engineering, and mathematics*. Washington, DC: National Academies Press.

National Research Council. (2013). *Next Generation Science Standards: For states, by states*. Washington, DC: The National Academies Press. doi: 10.17226/18290

Nordstrom, K., & Korpelainen, P. (2011) Creativity and inspiration for problem solving in engineering education. *Teaching in Higher Education, 16*(4), 439–450.

Partnership for 21st Century Skills. (n.d.) *Framework for 21st century learning*. Washington, DC: Author. Retrieved September 12, 2013 from http://www.p21.org/

Pearson. (2014, February 6). *Designing your open digital badge ecosystem* [Webinar]. Hosted by *The Chronicle of Higher Education*.

Remake Learning. (2015). *Remake learning playbook*. Retrieved from http://remakelearning.org/playbook/

Resnick, M., & Rosenbaum, E. (2013) Designing for tinkerability. In M. Honey & D. Kanter (Eds.), *Design, make, play: Growing the next generation of STEM innovators* (pp. 163–181). New York: Routledge.

Robinson, K. (2006). *Sir Ken Robinson: Do schools kill creativity?* TED Ideas Worth Spreading. Retrieved October 21, 2015 from https://www.ted.com/talks/ken_robinson_says_schools_kill_creativity?language=en

Schulman, K. (2013, March 27). White House hangout: The Maker Movement. [Web log post]. Retrieved from https://www.whitehouse.gov/blog/2013/03/27/white-house-hangout-maker-movement

Sheninger, E. (2014). *Digital leadership*. Thousand Oaks, CA: Corwin.

Shull, F. (2011). Protection from wishful thinking. *IEEE Software*, 28(4), 3–6.

Sousa, D. A., & Pilecki, T. (2013). *From STEM to STEAM: Using brain-compatible strategies to integrate the arts*. Thousand Oaks, CA: Corwin.

Stewart, L. (2014). Maker Movement reinvents education. *Newsweek*. Retrieved from http://www.newsweek.com/2014/09/19/maker-movement-reinvents-education-268739.html

U.S. National Commission on Excellence in Education. (1983). *A nation at risk: The imperative for educational reform: A report to the Nation and the Secretary of Education, United States Department of Education*. Washington, DC: Author.

Zhao, Y. (2012). *World class learners: Educating creative and entrepreneurial students*. Thousand Oaks, CA: Corwin.

Index

A SAGE Publishing Company

CORWIN HAS ONE MISSION: to enhance education through intentional professional learning.

We build long-term relationships with our authors, educators, clients, and associations who partner with us to develop and continuously improve the best evidence-based practices that establish and support lifelong learning.

Solutions you want. Experts you trust. Results you need.